THE BIBLE STORY

VOLUME II

—•—

MIGHTY MEN OF OLD

(From Jacob to the Dedication of Aaron)

The BIBLE STORY

More Than Four Hundred Stories in Ten Volumes
Covering the Entire Bible From Genesis to Revelation

VOLUME TWO
Mighty Men of Old

BY ARTHUR S. MAXWELL

Author of *Uncle Arthur's Bedtime Stories, The Children's Hour With Uncle Arthur,
The Secret of the Cave,* etc.

•

REVIEW AND HERALD PUBLISHING ASSOCIATION
Washington, D.C.

CONTENTS

Part I—Stories of Jacob, Esau, and Joseph

Part II—Stories of Israel in Egypt

When Jacob made Joseph a beautiful coat of many colors as a sign of his affection, it excited the envy of all Joseph's brothers and they began to plot how they might destroy him.

Part III—Stories of the Exodus

EXODUS 11:1-18:27

Part IV—Stories of Moses and the Tabernacle

EXODUS 19:1-LEVITICUS 8:36

PART I

Stories of Jacob, Esau, and Joseph
(Genesis 25:19-50:26)

STORY 1

So Much for So Little

LIKE his father, Isaac had to wait a long time for a son of his own—sixty years, in fact—and then he got two at once!

You can imagine the excitement among all the servants in the camp when twins were born to their master. Soon everybody was talking about the two little boys, Esau and Jacob. They especially liked the story of how Jacob, who was born last, grabbed his little brother's heel in his own tiny hand. They took this to be a sign that he would become more important than his brother, and strangely this is how it turned out.

To understand this story properly, you must remember that in those days the first boy in a family became heir to a double share of his father's property. So, because Esau was born a few minutes before Jacob, this "birthright" was his.

Those few minutes made all the difference between riches and poverty, honor and no honor. The second son just didn't count, any more than the third, fourth, or fifth. Even today in

9

← PAINTING BY PAUL B. REMMEY   ©   BY REVIEW AND HERALD

While they were quite young boys, Esau and Jacob were different in character. Esau liked to hunt with his bow and arrow, but Jacob preferred to stay at home and tend the sheep.

some countries the same custom is followed, and both title and estate all go to the eldest son upon a father's death.

But while being the first-born in any family meant a great deal, being Isaac's first-born meant much more, for this child would inherit not only most of his father's fortune but also all the blessings promised by God to Abraham.

Esau, therefore, was a very fortunate boy. By the lucky chance of being born first, both wealth and honor were his by right.

Strangely, however, it didn't mean a thing to him. He wasn't even interested. All he thought about was having a good time out in the fields and woods with his bow and arrows. It meant far more to him to be known as a cunning hunter and a good shot than as the first-born son of Isaac.

Jacob was different. He didn't like hunting, and preferred to stay around the house, where his mother told him stories of his father and grandfather and of the promises God had made to them. He especially liked the story about what happened at his birth when the Lord had said, "The elder shall serve the younger." He didn't understand what this meant at first, but as he thought about it he began to wonder how he could get the birthright away from his brother.

Because he stayed home more than Esau, his mother came to love him best, and what with one thing and another the two boys gradually drew apart.

This was a great pity, for surely twins were meant to love each other in a special way all through life. How much better it would have been for both of them had they played and worked

10

together, with Jacob sharing the fun in the woods and Esau staying home a bit more to help around the house and enjoy his mother's stories!

But it didn't work out that way. Soon both boys were treating each other like strangers.

One day Esau came home from the fields feeling very hungry. As he strode toward the house there was nothing he wanted in all the world so much as something to eat. And whom should he see but Jacob getting the dinner ready.

"Mother's boy, doing the cooking now!" he may have thought, but he didn't say it. He wanted food too badly.

"What have you got there?" I can hear him saying.

"Lentils," replies Jacob, continuing to stir the pot.

"Give me some," says Esau. "I'm near fainting."

But Jacob is in a mean frame of mind. Seeing his brother desperately hungry, he thinks this may be his chance to get the birthright away from him. So he refuses to give Esau any food unless he promises to trade with him.

"Trade?" Esau asks in surprise. "Trade what?"

"How about selling me the birthright for a nice, big bowl of lentils?"

"It's a deal," says Esau carelessly, grabbing for the bowl with never a thought of the consequences of what he has said.

So that Esau could never get out of the bargain, Jacob says to him, "Swear to me this day; and he sware unto him: and he sold his birthright unto Jacob. Then Jacob gave Esau bread and pottage of lentiles; and he did eat and drink, and rose up, and went his way: thus Esau despised his birthright."

11

Afterward, of course, Esau realized what he had done and how much he had given away for one dish of lentils. All his father's riches, the privilege of being head of the house after his father's death, the honor of being the one through whom the promises of God would be fulfilled—through whom Jesus, the Messiah, at last should come. All this he had valued at a few cents, the price of "one morsel of meat."

So much for so little!

He was very sad about it and wept a great deal, begging Jacob to go back on the deal and leave things as they were before. But Jacob refused.

As the Bible says, Esau despised his birthright, made light of something of great spiritual importance, and now "he found no place of repentance, though he sought it carefully with tears."

All of us—you and I and everybody—have to be careful not to make the same mistake. For we too have a "birthright." We may be "heirs of God, and joint-heirs with Christ" if we want to be. All the treasures of heaven will be ours if we are faithful to God and never deny Him. Indeed, He has said that He will gladly let us live forever with Him if only we will love Him truly all our days.

So much has He promised us! Let us make sure we never exchange these precious blessings for some little passing pleasure. Our birthright is too rich a treasure to sell for a mess of pottage.

STORY 2

Cheating Never Pays

ESAU did not forgive Jacob for cheating him out of his birthright. As for Jacob, he wasn't very happy about it either, because he never felt quite sure that the hard bargain he had made with his brother would be honored by his father. Back of his mind all the time was the thought that Isaac would ignore the deal as just a boyish prank, and so the birthright would belong to Esau after all.

Year after year the brothers drifted farther and farther apart, with Esau turning more and more to his hunting, and Jacob to things around the camp.

Meanwhile Isaac was growing old, and his sight was failing. Thinking he was going to die, he sent for Esau, intending to give him a special parting blessing—just as though the birthright still belonged to him.

As Esau came into the tent Isaac said to him, "My son: . . . Behold now, I am old, I know not the day of my death: now therefore take, I pray thee, thy weapons, thy quiver and thy bow, and go out to the field, and hunt me some venison; and make me savoury meat, such as I love, and bring it to me, that I may eat; that my soul may bless thee before I die."

Glad to be able to do something for his father, and happier still that the old man wasn't going to let Jacob get away with the birthright after all, Esau hurried out, picked up his bow and arrows, and went off to hunt. But, sad to say, Rebekah had overheard what Isaac had said about blessing Esau on his return. Guessing what he meant to do, and that her precious Jacob wasn't going to have the best of everything after all, she quickly thought up a scheme to get her own way.

Finding Jacob, she told him what had happened, and suggested that, seeing Isaac was so nearly blind, it would be easy to deceive him.

"Obey my voice," she said firmly. "Go now to the flock, and fetch me from thence two good kids of the goats; and I will make them savoury meat for thy father, such as he loveth: and thou shalt bring it to thy father, that he may eat, and that he may bless thee before his death."

At first Jacob didn't want to do it. He was scared. Not because he thought his mother's idea was wrong, but in case he might be found out.

"Esau my brother," he said, "is a hairy man, and I am a smooth man: my father peradventure will feel me, and I shall seem to him as a deceiver; and I shall bring a curse upon me, and not a blessing."

Rebekah, however, had set her heart on Jacob's getting that blessing, and finally talked him into doing what she wanted.

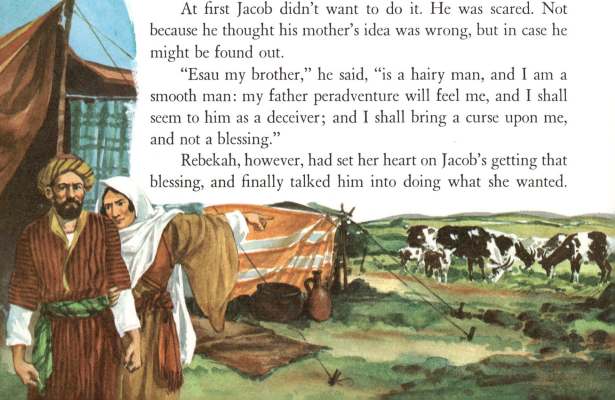

So Jacob fetched the two kids, and his mother made the kind of meal she knew Isaac loved.

Then she dressed Jacob in some of Esau's best clothes, and to complete the deception, put part of the skins of the kids on his hands and neck, where his father might possibly stroke him.

What a sham he was when he went into his father's tent with that steaming plate of food! And how frightened he must have felt lest Isaac should discover his wicked trickery! It's a wonder he didn't spill the gravy all over the place. But he felt worse still when Isaac began to act suspicious.

"Who art thou, my son?" asked the old man, trying hard to see who had come into his tent.

"I am Esau thy firstborn," Jacob said, trying to make his voice sound like Esau's. "I have done according as thou badest me: arise, I pray thee, sit and eat of my venison, that thy soul may bless me."

Now Isaac became even more suspicious.

"How is it that thou hast found it so quickly, my son?" he asked.

"Because the Lord thy God brought it to me," said Jacob, making his crime worse by bringing God into it.

By this time Isaac was more sure than ever that something was wrong.

"Come near, I pray thee, that I may feel thee, my son, whether thou be my very son Esau or not."

Jacob moved toward his father, probably shivering in his shoes lest he be found out.

Isaac began to feel him all over. He was puzzled.

15

"The voice is Jacob's voice," he said, "but the hands are the hands of Esau."

He paused a moment, then said again, "*Art* thou my very son Esau?"

And Jacob, lying to the last, replied, "I am."

Satisfied, Isaac ate the food Jacob had brought, afterward blessing him, saying, among other things, "Let people serve thee, and nations bow down to thee: be lord over thy brethren, and let thy mother's sons bow down to thee."

No doubt Isaac had been thinking for days about all the good things he would promise his eldest son, so dear to him. Now he said them all to the wrong boy!

The blessing received, Jacob hurried out, tore off Esau's clothes, and tried to look as innocent as he could. But if he thought his brother wouldn't find out, he was greatly mistaken.

Hardly had Jacob left the tent than Esau returned.

That was a sad, sad moment.

"And it came to pass, as soon as Isaac had made an end of blessing Jacob, and Jacob was yet scarce gone out from the presence of Isaac his father, that Esau his brother came in from his hunting."

Never dreaming that anything had gone wrong, he went on making the savory meal, then happily carried it to his father.

"Let my father arise," he said, "and eat of his son's venison, that thy soul may bless me."

Then the blow fell.

"Who art thou?" demanded his father in a loud voice, angry that anyone should play with him like this.

2-2

← PAINTED AFTER DORÉ   ©   BY REVIEW AND HERALD

With his mother's help Jacob put hairy skins over his arms and neck to deceive his blind father Isaac, so that he might receive the blessing intended for his older brother, Esau.

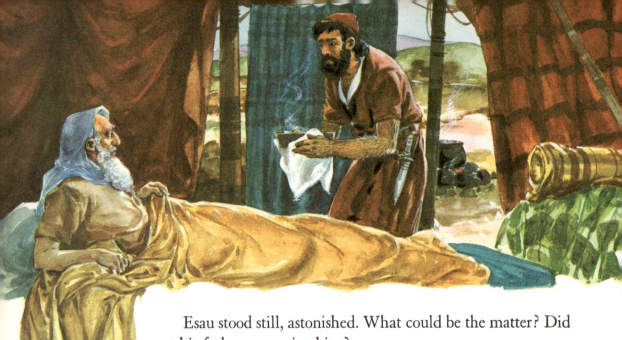

Esau stood still, astonished. What could be the matter? Did not his father recognize him?

"I am thy son, thy firstborn Esau."

"Who?" cried Isaac, now trembling all over. "Who? where is he that hath taken venison, and brought it me, and I have eaten of all before thou camest, and have blessed him?"

Esau was heartbroken. What he had thought might be his last labor of love for his dear old father had been completely spoiled. The food he had so carefully prepared with his own hands was not wanted. And now the blessing he had been promised had been given to someone else. It was too much. He broke down and wept, crying out in his sorrow, "Bless me, even me also, O my father."

No more pitiful words were ever spoken. But what could Isaac do? He had given the blessing to Jacob, and according to the custom of those days, he could not take it back.

He gave Esau another blessing, truly, but it wasn't just the same, and Esau knew it.

"And Esau hated Jacob because of the blessing wherewith

18

his father blessed him: and Esau said in his heart, The days of mourning for my father are at hand; then will I slay my brother Jacob."

He not only said it "in his heart." He told his friends, and someone passed it on to Rebekah, and she told Jacob.

Of course, from the first Jacob had been afraid that this might happen; now he became more frightened than ever, and decided that his only safety lay in flight.

Rebekah suggested that he flee to his Uncle Laban's home in Haran, and this he agreed to do.

"Tarry with him a few days," she said, "until thy brother's fury turn away; . . . and he forget that which thou hast done to him: then I will send, and fetch thee from thence: why should I be deprived also of you both in one day?"

Little did she know of the future, or of the price both she and her son would pay for this miserable deed.

"In one day" she did indeed lose both her boys—and broke her own heart. For Esau hated her, and Jacob she never saw again.

She expected him back in a few days, but he never returned while she was alive.

As for Jacob, he lost both his home and his mother. For years he suffered great loneliness and disappointment, and was never free from fear and remorse for what he had done.

Some boys and girls today think that cheating is smart. But it isn't. If you have any doubts, think about Jacob and the price he had to pay for being so mean and selfish. Cheating never pays.

19

STORY 3

The Ladder From Earth
to Heaven

≈≈≈≈≈≈≈≈≈≈≈≈≈≈≈≈

THAT last night Jacob spent in his old home must have been anything but a happy one.

Esau was furious. Jacob was afraid. Everybody in the camp guessed that something terrible had happened.

Rebekah went to see Isaac and tried to put the best light possible on what Jacob had done. Then she changed the subject.

"Jacob needs to get married," she said, and went on to tell how she was worried lest he should become interested in one of the daughters of Heth. "If Jacob take a wife of the daughters of Heth, such as these which are of the daughters of the land, what good shall my life do me?"

Isaac agreed with her that Jacob should go to his mother's home in Haran and find a wife among the daughters of his uncle Laban. This suited Rebekah very well, because now she would not have to tell people the real reason why Jacob was leaving home so suddenly.

20

Then Jacob was called in and told what he was to do. And the Bible says, "Jacob obeyed his father and his mother, and was gone."

"And was gone." How much sadness there is in those three words! His mother's tears. His father's worry. His own heartbreak. All the awful loneliness of separation. What a price to pay for wrongdoing!

Sick of heart, and miserable beyond words, Jacob trudged along under the stars on the trail that led to Haran. No camels for him such as Eliezer had taken when he went to find a wife for Isaac. He was in disgrace, and he knew it.

The more he thought about what he had done, the more he despised himself. What a fool he had been! How much he had lost, and how little he had gained! He might be in name the heir to his father's riches, but here he was, penniless, fleeing for his life from his own twin brother.

At last, weary and homesick, he flung himself upon the ground, hoping that sleep would cause him to forget his fears and sorrows. None of the comforts he enjoyed at home were his now. He had only the hard ground to lie on, and "he took of the stones of that place, and put them for his pillows, and lay down in that place to sleep."

Never did he feel so low, so wretched, so far from God as at that moment; yet, strangely enough, never was God so near.

As he slept he dreamed, "and behold a ladder set up on the earth, and the top of it reached to heaven: and behold the angels of God ascending and descending on it.

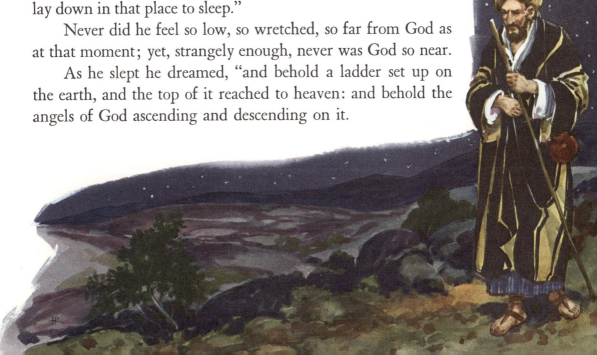

"And, behold, the Lord stood above it, and said, I am the Lord God of Abraham thy father, and the God of Isaac: the land whereon thou liest, to thee will I give it, and to thy seed; and thy seed shall be as the dust of the earth, and thou shalt spread abroad to the west, and to the east, and to the north, and to the south: and in thee and in thy seed shall all the families of the earth be blessed. And, behold, I am with thee, and will keep thee in all places whither thou goest, and will bring thee again into this land; for I will not leave thee, until I have done that which I have spoken to thee of.

"And Jacob awaked out of his sleep, and he said, Surely the Lord is in this place; and I knew it not."

How could God have spoken like this to such a mean, low-down fellow? Didn't He know how bad Jacob had been? Yes, God knew everything about him. But the most wonderful thing about God is that He is always willing to forgive even the worst of sinners. To the meanest and the most selfish, to all the Jacobs in the world, He says, "Come now, and let us reason together, . . . though your sins be as scarlet, they shall be as white as snow; though they be red like crimson, they shall be as wool."

And this is what God was trying to say that night to Jacob as he slept with his head on a rock. "Look up!" He tried to say to this wayward youth. "There's a way back. There's a ladder from earth to heaven, and you can climb it."

As Jacob awoke, and he began to think about his dream, his heart was touched, and he cried out amid his tears, "This is none other but the house of God, and this is the gate of heaven."

22

THE LADDER FROM EARTH TO HEAVEN

And it must have seemed just like that to him, with that wonderful shining ladder stretching far up into the sky, with the angels moving up and down upon it, and the glory of the Lord above it, and His voice speaking such kind and tender words.

As Jacob thought of God's kindness and mercy he made up his mind that from that moment on he would live a better life. And he made God a promise, saying, "If God will be with me, and will keep me in this way that I go, and will give me bread to eat, and raiment to put on, so that I come again to my father's house in peace; then shall the Lord be my God: . . . and of all that thou shalt give me I will surely give the tenth unto thee."

It was the prayer of a worried, hungry, homesick man taking his first faltering step toward heaven, but God was glad for it and accepted it. So too He rejoices when any one of us comes back to Him, no matter in what words we tell Him we are sorry for our sins.

Yes! That ladder from earth to heaven was God's way of telling us all that no matter how bad we may have been, we may come back to Him anytime we want to. How very wonderful it is that there is a ladder leading from just where we are right up to the throne of glory!

Is that ladder really there? It is. You may see it in your dreams tonight. You may climb it when you will. For that ladder is none other than Jesus, who once said to Nathanael, "Hereafter ye shall see heaven open, and the angels of God ascending and descending upon the Son of man."

Yes, Jesus is the ladder up to heaven. He is "the way, the truth, and the life: no man cometh unto the Father," but by Him.

When we know we have done wrong, and feel just as low as Jacob did when he lay on that pile of stones, we may think again of that beautiful ladder and see it going straight up from our tear-stained pillow into heaven. And above it we may see the glory of God and know He is waiting to forgive, waiting to say, "Behold, I am with thee, and will keep thee . . . ; for I will not leave thee."

Did you do something wrong today? Were you cross, unkind, ugly, deceitful? Are you sorry? Do you want to be good? The ladder is beside you. Use it. Climb back to God right now!

STORY 4

A Long, Long Lesson

≈≈≈≈≈≈≈≈≈≈≈≈≈≈

AFTER many long, hot days of walking, and many sad and lonely nights lying on the hard ground, Jacob at last drew near his journey's end.

He was now in his mother's country—the land she had told him about so many times in his childhood. Now he was seeing it for the first time.

One morning, as he trudged along in the warm sunshine, "he looked, and behold a well in the field, and, lo, there were three flocks of sheep lying by it; . . . and a great stone was upon the well's mouth."

Glad to have someone to talk to after being alone so long, Jacob went over to the shepherds and spoke to them.

"To which city do you belong?" he asked.

"Haran," they replied.

"Then you know Laban, the son of Nahor?" asked Jacob.

"We know him," they said.

"Is he well?"

"He's well," replied the shepherds, "and, behold, Rachel his daughter cometh with the sheep."

Eagerly Jacob looked at the beautiful girl coming toward the well with a flock of her father's sheep. Forgetting that it was now high noon, and that nobody was supposed to open the well till evening, he rolled away the heavy stone and began to draw water for Rachel's sheep.

Never had a lowly task like this seemed so pleasant to him. Indeed, it didn't seem to take any time at all, not with this lovely girl smiling at him. How like his mother she was!

The watering finished, he ran over to Rachel, kissed her, and burst into tears! Then he told her that he was her Aunt Rebekah's son, and she was so excited she ran home at once and told her father. Laban came hurrying out, and when he saw Jacob he "embraced him, and kissed him, and brought him to his house."

Jacob spent a very happy month in Laban's home, and

when his uncle suggested he stay longer and work for him, Jacob said he would. Then Laban asked him what wages he would expect.

"Just Rachel," he said. He wanted no other reward, he loved her so much. "I will serve thee seven years for Rachel thy younger daughter."

Laban agreed, and "Jacob served seven years for Rachel; and they seemed unto him but a few days, for the love he had to her."

Jacob worked very hard for his uncle. As he said later, "In the day the drought consumed me, and the frost by night; and my sleep departed from mine eyes." Yet none of these hardships mattered. He felt he could endure anything just so he could have Rachel for his wife.

The seven years drew to a close. Everything seemed to be going well. The wedding day was fixed, and Laban arranged for the feast.

Then Jacob suffered the biggest disappointment any man could have. By a crafty trick that, for downright meanness, matched Jacob's deception of his old father, Laban married him to his oldest daughter Leah instead of to Rachel.

You can imagine how angry Jacob was when he discovered he had been tricked. "What is this you have done to me?" he cried. "Didn't I serve you for Rachel? Why have you deceived me like this?"

He didn't want Leah. In fact, he disliked her. There was something the matter with her eyes. Maybe that's why she hadn't married before. But under the law of the land he could not get rid of her.

Poor Jacob! He was learning something he needed to know—what it feels like to be cheated. By a long, long lesson he was being taught that it never pays to lie and deceive.

And now we see Laban's character a little more clearly. He was a hard bargainer, if ever there was one. Yes, he told Jacob, he would keep his word to let him have Rachel, but he would require seven more years of service.

Seven more years! It didn't seem fair, but Jacob agreed to his uncle's terms. There wasn't much else he could do.

When the second seven years were up Jacob decided to leave and return to his old home in Canaan. He had had enough.

"Give me my wives and my children," he said, "and let me go."

But Laban knew when he was well off, and begged him to stay. "For I have learned by experience that the Lord hath blessed me for thy sake," he said.

A LONG, LONG LESSON

Once more Jacob agreed to stay, this time for wages. But the next six years were not happy ones. True, he now had flocks and herds of his own, and these seemed to multiply more rapidly than Laban's, but Laban kept changing his wages. Then, too, Laban's sons became more and more jealous of Jacob. They thought he was getting rich at their expense.

So he talked it all over with Rachel and Leah, and they agreed that it would be better for everybody if they should pack up and leave, even if they had to go without telling Laban.

Then one night the Lord appeared to Jacob and said, "I am the God of Bethel, where thou anointedst the pillar, and where thou vowedst a vow unto me: now arise, get thee out from this land, and return unto the land of thy kindred."

This touched Jacob's heart, for Bethel was the place where, twenty years before, he had seen the ladder reaching up from earth to heaven. How wonderful, he thought, that God still remembered the vow he made that night to live a better life!

Now Jacob was quite sure he should leave Laban and go back to his old home.

"Then Jacob rose up, and set his sons and his wives upon camels; and he carried away all his cattle, and all his goods which he had gotten, . . . to go to Isaac his father in the land of Canaan. . . .

"And Jacob stole away unawares to Laban the Syrian, in that he told him not that he fled."

Hurrying as fast as possible, he ferried his family and his property over the river Euphrates and made for Mount Gilead on the border of Canaan.

Jacob got a good start on his uncle, for it was not until the third day that Laban heard what had happened. Now it was Laban's turn to feel tricked, and he didn't like it. Gathering a band of men, he pursued after Jacob, determined to bring him back. But on the way God spoke to him in a dream and said, "Take heed that thou speak not to Jacob from good to bad." God knew that this was just what Laban was likely to do, start out with pleasant words and end up with angry ones, as so many people do.

Meanwhile, Jacob drove on as fast as he could, but with so large a family and so many cattle, it was impossible to keep ahead. At last, after a wild seven days' chase, Laban caught up with him at Mount Gilead.

"What hast thou done," cried Laban, as he came puffing up to Jacob, "that thou hast stolen away unawares to me, and carried away my daughters, as captives taken with the sword? Wherefore didst thou flee away secretly, and steal away from me; and didst not tell me, that I might have sent thee away with mirth, and with songs, with tabret, and with harp? And hast not suffered me to kiss my sons and my daughters?"

Jacob knew that Laban had never intended to let him go and that all this about making a farewell feast for him was just so much talk. So he gave Laban a piece of his mind. After reminding him of all his long and faithful service, he said, "Thus have I been twenty years in thy house; I served thee fourteen years for thy two daughters, and six years for thy cattle: and thou hast changed my wages ten times. Except the God of my father, the God of Abraham, and the fear of Isaac, had been with me, surely thou hadst sent me away now empty. God hath seen mine affliction and the labour of my hands, and rebuked thee yesternight."

Laban began to cool off. Seeing that Jacob was determined to go back to Canaan, and there was nothing he could do about it, he suggested that they make peace. Jacob agreed, and as was the custom in those days, they all began piling up stones to form some sort of memorial. Laban called it "Mizpah," meaning "a beacon, or watchtower," saying, "The Lord watch between me and thee, when we are absent one from another." It was a happy ending to what might have been a very serious quarrel.

Early next morning they bade each other farewell, and Laban "kissed his sons and his daughters, and blessed them," and went back home.

STORY 5

Struggle in the Night

JACOB'S long, long lesson wasn't over yet. He had much more to learn before he could become the truly great man God wanted him to be.

No sooner was he out of one trouble than he was into another. As he waved good-by to his uncle Laban, he began to worry about Esau and what would happen if they met again.

That night, as he went on his way, "the angels of God met him." This cheered his heart, for they reminded him of the angels he had seen on the ladder up to heaven. But next day he was worrying again.

Finally he decided to send messengers to Esau to find out whether he had got over his anger during the past twenty years. But when the messengers returned a few days later they brought news that Esau had not changed his mind at all. Instead he was as determined as ever to take vengeance on the one who had swindled him so badly.

"We came to thy brother Esau," said the messengers, "and also he cometh to meet thee, and four hundred men with him."

STRUGGLE IN THE NIGHT

Four hundred men! What could Jacob do against so many? No wonder he became "greatly afraid and distressed." All he could think of doing was to divide his caravan into two parts, so that if Esau should "come to the one company, and smite it" there was just a chance the other might escape. It wasn't much of a way out, and he knew it.

In his anxiety he turned to God. "O God of my father Abraham," he cried, "and God of my father Isaac, the Lord which saidst unto me, Return unto thy country, and to thy kindred, and I will deal well with thee: I am not worthy of the least of all the mercies, and of all the truth, which thou hast shewed unto thy servant; for with my staff I passed over this Jordan; and now I am become two bands.

"Deliver me, I pray thee, from the hand of my brother, from the hand of Esau: . . . and thou saidst, I will surely do thee good, and make thy seed as the sand of the sea, which cannot be numbered for multitude."

Jacob's prayer shows how much he had grown in grace during his long, hard years with Laban. Now he was grateful for all that God had done for him, and given him, since he left home with nothing but a staff in his hand.

Most important of all, he was humble at last and willing to admit that he was unworthy of the least of God's mercies.

That night, having sent his family over the brook Jabbok to what seemed the safest place in sight, Jacob was left alone. He wanted to be alone. He felt a great need to talk with God all by himself. So there in the dark and the silence he flung himself on his knees, confessed his sins, and asked again for help.

2-3

STRUGGLE IN THE NIGHT

Suddenly he felt himself gripped by strong hands, and started up in terror. Perhaps one of Esau's men had found him, or possibly some roving robber had crept up on him. He struggled to get free. But it was not easy. His thigh went out of joint, and he was in great pain. Yet he wrestled on till daybreak.

And then it was that the wonderful truth dawned upon Jacob that it was no common thief with whom he had been struggling, nor one of Esau's men, but the Lord Himself. Like so many of us today, he had been in the very arms of God and had not realized it.

Now, instead of trying to break away, he held on, crying, "I will not let thee go, except thou bless me."

And the Lord said, "What is thy name?"

"Jacob," he said meekly, the name meaning "supplanter," or cheat.

"Thy name shall be called no more Jacob, but Israel [meaning, A prince of God]: for as a prince hast thou power with God and with men, and hast prevailed."

And Jacob called that place "Peniel," meaning "the face of God," for, he said, "I have seen God face to face, and my life is preserved. And as he passed over Penuel the sun rose upon him."

It was indeed the dawn of a new day for Jacob. He had passed the great turning point of his life. He had found God for himself at last. His fears were gone. Courage and hope filled his heart. He was a new man. The coward, the cheat, the swindler, had become a prince of God.

It was like walking out of darkness into sunshine.

35

In the early morning Jacob found himself wrestling with an angel of God, whose power he could not overcome. Tired and lame, Jacob then pleaded with the angel for his blessing.

STORY 6

The Twins Make Peace

HAVING made peace with God, Jacob's one desire was to make peace with his brother.

He had told God he was sorry for his sins, and now he was ready to tell Esau the same thing. There was no pride in his heart any more, or any desire to cheat or deceive. He was now a "prince of God," and wanted to do right.

His first thought was to send a present to Esau as a token of his love. And this is what he sent:

"Two hundred she goats, and twenty he goats, two hundred ewes, and twenty rams, thirty milch camels with their colts, forty kine, and ten bulls, twenty she asses, and ten foals."

There was nothing mean or little about a present like this. It would be a costly gift today, and it surely was then.

Jacob sent the animals forward, drove by drove, telling the servants in charge of each drove to say, when they met Esau, "This is a present from Jacob and, behold, he is behind us."

36

THE TWINS MAKE PEACE

Jacob's idea was to impress Esau with the greatness of his gift as he should see one drove after another coming toward him. "I will appease him with the present that goeth before me," he said, "and afterward I will see his face; peradventure he will accept of me."

Just in case the present, big as it was, might not be enough to soften Esau's heart, Jacob arranged for the women and children to follow next. In front he put the handmaids with their children, then Leah with her six little boys, and Dinah, her daughter. And finally dear Rachel with her precious Joseph.

As the caravan moved slowly onward in its new order someone up ahead raised the cry, "Esau is coming!" and the word was passed back from one to another, leaving everybody much afraid. Everybody, that is, except Jacob. He wasn't afraid any more. Brave in the new strength he had received from God, he walked boldly forward, past his wives and children, and "bowed himself to the ground seven times" as he came nearer and nearer to his brother. He could

not have done more to show that he was truly sorry for what he had done, and that he wanted to be friends again.

Esau's anger melted away at sight of his brother kneeling to him, and "he ran to meet him, and embraced him, and fell on his neck, and kissed him: and they wept."

What a lovely meeting! And how beautiful that they should have kissed each other! How happy it must have made all the women and children, and all Esau's men too! I wouldn't be surprised if a lot of those people were wiping their eyes as the long-separated twins met and made peace.

Esau then asked about all the women and children in Jacob's party, and one by one they came up and were introduced.

Then he asked, "What were all those droves I met on the way?"

"These are to find grace in the sight of my lord," said Jacob, smiling between his tears.

"I have enough, my brother," said Esau, thanking him. "Keep them for yourself."

But Jacob pressed him to accept the present, and Esau at last agreed to do so.

There was something very fine about Esau, for now he offered to go ahead of Jacob's caravan with his four hundred men, as a bodyguard for the rest of the journey.

THE TWINS MAKE PEACE

Jacob thanked him, but said there was no need for him to do that. And, anyway, the bodyguard might want to move too quickly.

"My lord knoweth that the children are tender," he said, "and the flocks and herds with young are with me: and if men should overdrive them one day, all the flock will die. . . . I will lead on softly, according as the cattle that goeth before me and the children be able to endure."

Esau saw the wisdom of this, but he was so anxious to do something for his brother that he offered to leave some of his men with Jacob to help with the work.

Again Jacob thanked him, but said it wasn't necessary; he would be all right.

Then, with many smiles, and kisses, and handshakes, the brothers parted again, this time in peace, with everything forgiven.

As Esau and his men rode away I expect they kept turning round to wave their hands in farewell. And Jacob waved too. And Leah, and Rachel. And all the children. How they waved their little hands over and over again!

Such a happy parting it was this time, so different from that other one twenty years before.

STORY 7

Sold Into Slavery

MOVING slowly along, Jacob and his caravan came at last to a place called Shalem. As everybody was tired of traveling, and the place looked rather nice, he decided to settle there. So he bought a piece of land just outside the city for one hundred lambs, and set up camp.

But it didn't work out well. Some of his children got into very serious trouble with the children of the city, and God told Jacob to move away from there to Bethel.

"Dwell there," the Lord said to him; "and make there an altar unto God, that appeared unto thee when thou fleddest from the face of Esau thy brother."

There was need for them all to remember God. Things had been slipping. Some of Jacob's servants had been getting interested in the idols that the people of the land were worshiping. The girls too were dressing themselves up with ornaments, just like the heathen. They all needed to get back to Bethel, to "the house of God" and "the gate of heaven."

40

SOLD INTO SLAVERY

"Then Jacob said unto his household, and to all that were with him, Put away the strange gods that are among you, and be clean, and change your garments. . . . And they gave unto Jacob all the strange gods which were in their hand, and all their earrings which were in their ears."

For a while there was quite a reformation.

Then something very sad happened. Rachel died. Just as she was having her second baby too. Jacob was heartbroken, for he loved Rachel best of all.

As she was dying Rachel named her baby Benoni, meaning "son of my sorrow," but Jacob changed it to Benjamin, meaning "son of the right hand," which showed how much he thought of him. From now on Rachel's two boys, Joseph and Benjamin, became specially precious to their sorrowing father.

Jacob now had twelve sons, and you really should know all their names. Here they are:

Reuben, Simeon, Levi, Judah, Issachar, Zebulun, Joseph, Benjamin, Dan, Naphtali, Gad, Asher.

Besides all these boys, there was Dinah, and possibly other daughters whose names we do not know, making a very large family altogether. No wonder Jacob needed such large flocks and herds to feed them all!

As was the custom in those days, the boys all helped with the farm chores, spending much of their time minding the sheep and looking after the other animals belonging to their father. They were shepherds, cowboys, and farmers all in one. And a husky lot they were, as you can imagine.

Somehow Joseph did not fit in with his older brothers. They looked on him as "little brother" and a bit of a nuisance. Once he told his father some of the bad things they were saying and doing, and they found out about it. After that they didn't like to have him around lest he should tell on them again.

Because Joseph was Rachel's son, Jacob favored him more than the others, and this helped to make things worse. One day he had a beautiful coat made for Joseph. It was of many colors and made him stand out from all the rest. At this the older brothers became more jealous of him than ever. Quite likely they said their father had never given them coats as good as that. They began to be suspicious too that Jacob might be planning to give the birthright to Joseph instead of to Reuben.

One day Joseph told his brothers about a dream he had had. He said they were all binding sheaves of corn in a field when suddenly all their sheaves bowed down to his sheaf. You can imagine how they liked that!

Then he told them of another dream—how the sun, moon, and eleven stars bowed down to him; and they liked that still less.

Joseph might have been wiser to have kept these dreams to himself, or told them only to his father. But the fact that he told them to his brothers shows how innocent he really was. He never thought they would mind. Perhaps he hoped they would tell him what the dreams meant.

But the ten bigger brothers did mind. Very much. They had no intention of bowing down to this little sneak, as they thought he was. Soon they became so angry with him they even talked of killing him.

One day, when Joseph was seventeen, his brothers saw him coming toward them across the fields and "they said one to another, Behold, this dreamer cometh. Come now therefore, and let us slay him, and cast him into some pit, and we will say, Some evil beast hath devoured him: and we shall see what will become of his dreams."

Just then Reuben came on the scene and overheard what the others were suggesting. Although he disliked Joseph as much as the rest, he wasn't willing to go so far as to kill him. Being the eldest, he knew his father would hold him responsible.

"Let us not kill him," he said. "Shed no blood, but cast him into this pit," his purpose being to take Joseph out later and send him back home.

The others agreed, then waited for their brother to arrive.

Meanwhile Joseph, who had walked a long, long way—almost fifty miles—looking for his brothers, was feeling very happy that at last he had found them. At the joy of seeing them again he almost forgot how tired and hungry he was. Imagine, then, his disappointment when he saw the ugly looks on their faces. This was not the welcome he had expected. Then, to his horror, some of them seized him, tore off his precious coat of many colors, carried him to a deep pit, and threw him in.

In vain he cried to them to have mercy on him, but they wouldn't listen, and soon he found himself left alone at the bottom of the pit, hungry, cold, and heartbroken. He called and called, but no one came. For all he knew, he was to be left there to die of thirst and starvation.

Meanwhile Reuben had gone back to his work, and the others, left to themselves, started to talk about what to do with Joseph. They were in trouble. Having agreed not to kill the boy, they couldn't leave him in the pit to die; but if they let him go, he would surely run home and tell his father how cruel they had all been to him.

Just then they saw a caravan approaching, and discovered it was a company of Ishmaelites from Gilead "with their camels bearing spicery and balm and myrrh, going to carry it down to Egypt."

At this Judah had a bright idea. "Come," he said, "let us sell him to the Ishmaelites."

The very thing!

The rest agreed at once, for not only would this get them out of a very difficult situation, but they would make some money as well.

So the caravan was stopped, and the bargaining began. Finally Joseph was lifted out of the pit and, despite his tears

45

and pleadings, was sold to the Ishmaelites for twenty pieces of silver.

Thus within an hour or two of his arrival at his brothers' camp, poor Joseph, pride and joy of his father's heart, found himself a slave in a caravan bound for Egypt.

How cruel brothers can be sometimes! I hope you never have any thoughts like these about *your* little brother.

Looking back, we can see that their deed was not only wicked but very foolish. It brought them no good. The twenty pieces of silver didn't go far among ten. Just two pieces each, which were soon spent. What's more, they didn't actually get rid of Joseph, for after he was gone they couldn't get him out of their minds. They worried about what they had done and what might happen to them if they were ever found out. And there was always the possibility that they might meet Joseph again someday. Then there were those dreams of his. What did they mean?

Could it be that they had made a dreadful mistake? They surely had.

STORY 8

A Sad, Sad Journey

HARDLY had the Ishmaelites' caravan disappeared in the gathering dusk before Reuben returned to the pit to set Joseph free. Imagine how shocked he was to discover that the boy was no longer there!

Finding his brothers, he said in alarm, "The child is not; and I, whither shall I go?"

He couldn't bear the thought of facing his father without Joseph. It would break the old man's heart. And he simply couldn't tell him that they had all been mean and cruel enough to sell him as a slave!

Then someone suggested a way out. Jacob must be told a lie—that Joseph had been killed by some wild animal. To make the story seem true, they took Joseph's coat of many colors and dipped it in the blood of an animal and carried it to Jacob.

"This have we found," they said; "know now whether it be thy son's coat or no."

Jacob knew it, of course. No one but Joseph had ever owned a coat like that.

"It is my son's coat," he said with a sob; "an evil beast hath devoured him; Joseph is without doubt rent in pieces."

So Jacob, who had deceived his father, was now deceived by his own sons.

"And Jacob . . . mourned for his son many days. And all his sons and all his daughters rose up to comfort him; but he refused to be comforted; and he said, For I will go down into the grave unto my son mourning. Thus his father wept for him."

How those brothers could have tried to comfort their poor old father without once telling him the truth is more than I can imagine. And yet they dared not tell what they had done. If they had, their father's anger against them might have known no bounds.

Meanwhile poor Joseph, sad, weary, and homesick, was on his way to Egypt.

To think of it! Only seventeen, and sold as a slave!

As he trudged along the dusty trail with his Ishmaelite masters, many a tear must have run down his cheeks. Why, oh, why, had all this evil come upon him? he wondered. Why had his brothers been so cruel to him? Why had they let him be taken away by strangers like this? Why hadn't anybody come to his rescue?

As evening fell on that first night away from home, he must have felt terribly lonely. He couldn't help thinking about his comfortable bed at home, his pets, and all the things a boy cares for most. And then he must have thought of his father, and his precious little brother Benjamin, and his mother who had died. That made him cry again.

Joseph had never been away from home, but now he was sold by his cruel brothers as a slave to rough strangers, who took him far away from home over a hot, dusty road to Egypt.

What a sad, sad journey it was! For the nearer the caravan came to Egypt, the farther it got from home. Over and over again Joseph must have thought that he would never see his home any more. Many times he must have worried about what would happen to him in the foreign land to which he was being taken. That he would soon be sold to someone else, he was sure; but to whom? It might be to somebody very harsh and cruel, who would make his life miserable.

And then he thought of God, his father's God. And though the Bible doesn't actually say so, we may be sure he prayed many times that God would look after him and somehow help him to find his loved ones again someday.

We may be sure too that God was watching over this dear boy, just as He watches over every boy and girl who loves and trusts Him.

In His providence this sad journey into slavery was the best thing that could have happened to Joseph. Though the boy did not understand it at the time, God was using his brothers' unkindness to lead him to a great future which otherwise he would never have known.

God often does that, bringing great blessing and happiness out of something that for a while seems very hard to bear. He loves to lead His trusting children out of darkness into light.

And so Joseph came into Egypt, gazing wide eyed at its great cities, its huge temples, its mighty Pyramids, its mysterious Sphinx, and all the throngs of strange-looking people. Never for a moment did he dream that someday he would be ruler of all this wonderful country.

PART ONE

STORY 9

Two Strange Dreams

ANXIOUS to get rid of Joseph at a profit, the Ishmaelites sold him to Potiphar, captain of the guard in Pharaoh's court, who wanted a lad to help around his house.

And so it came about that the son of one of the richest men in Canaan, who but a few days before had enjoyed everything he wanted in his father's house, was now no more than a slave, at the beck and call of a heathen master.

It must have been very hard for poor Joseph to take, but he made up his mind, with God's help, to make the best of it. Whatever he was asked to do he did well and faithfully, and his pleasant manner soon endeared him to everybody around. Potiphar himself took a great fancy to him, and gradually gave him more and more important tasks to do. The Bible says, "His master saw that the Lord was with him, and that the Lord made all that he did to prosper in his hand."

Not a word reached him from his old home. Nobody came to set him free. He was on his own, alone in the world. But as

51

the days and weeks and years went by he tried hard to live a good, clean, upright life before the Egyptians. His honesty, truthfulness, and gracious spirit made a great impression on them. He was a faithful witness for God and the truths he had been taught in boyhood by his father and mother.

One day Potiphar told Joseph that from now on he would be the "overseer," or business manager, of all his affairs. This was quite a promotion for a slave, and Joseph must have been very happy about it. No doubt he decided to try still harder to please his master.

Soon his wisdom and his winning ways were making everything run with wonderful smoothness in Potiphar's household, and "the Lord blessed the Egyptian's house for Joseph's sake; and the blessing of the Lord was upon all that he had in the house, and in the field."

Potiphar was so pleased with Joseph that he "left all that he had in Joseph's hand; and he knew not ought he had, save the bread which he did eat."

Then, just as everything was going so well, terrible trouble came. Potiphar's wife accused Joseph, falsely, of doing some-

52

thing very wrong. Her story was untrue and most unfair, but her husband felt there was nothing else he could do but to order Joseph thrown into prison.

It was enough to break Joseph's heart. He knew he was innocent. He had taken a firm stand for the right. When enticed to do evil he had nobly said, "How . . . can I do this great wickedness, and sin against God?" And now here he was in prison, chained in a dungeon like a common criminal! All his trying to be a faithful witness for God seemed to have been in vain.

How hard it is to be misjudged, isn't it? Yet Joseph would not let himself despair. Night after night as he lay in his cell, the iron fetters hurting his feet, he remembered the story his father had told him of his struggle in the night, and how he had held on to God till the daybreak when the sunshine came again. And he made up his mind that he too would be a prince of God, and prevail.

Because of his decision to be faithful to the Lord whatever happened, "the Lord was with Joseph, and shewed him mercy, and gave him favour in the sight of the keeper of the prison."

What a fine young man he must have been to have made the same good impression on everybody, no matter where he was, even in prison!

He was a born leader too, and pretty soon the keeper of the prison placed him in charge of all the other prisoners, and trusted him so completely that he "looked not to any thing that was under his hand; because the Lord was with him, and that which he did, the Lord made it to prosper."

53

One day two new prisoners arrived. One was Pharaoh's chief butler and the other his chief baker. Just what they had done wrong we are not told. Probably it had something to do with the food and drink they had supplied to his majesty. Whatever it was, it had made Pharaoh angry, and he had ordered them put in prison.

Joseph was able to sympathize with them, for he knew what it was to be unjustly punished. His kindly nature led him to be friendly to them, and they liked him for it.

One morning, when he went to see them in their cell, he noticed that they were both looking very worried.

"Why do you look so sad today?" he asked cheerfully. "Anything wrong?"

Then they told him how they had both dreamed strange dreams and could not understand their meaning.

"Do not interpretations belong to God?" said Joseph. "Tell me them, I pray you." Thus he let them know that he was a servant of the God of heaven, the God who knows everything,

and who is willing to help His faithful children in every time of need.

Then the chief butler told his dream. It was about a vine which had three branches. Buds came on the branches, which opened into blossoms. Then came clusters of grapes, which ripened. Finally he picked the grapes, squeezed them into Pharaoh's cup, and put the cup in his hand.

It was a very simple dream, yet the butler was sure it had some important meaning.

"You are right," said Joseph. "It has. The three branches are three days: yet within three days shall Pharaoh lift up thine head, and restore thee unto thy place: and thou shalt deliver Pharaoh's cup into his hand, after the former manner when thou wast his butler."

You can imagine how pleased the chief butler was when he got this good news. All his sadness vanished. And he felt very thankful to Joseph for interpreting his dream like this.

Joseph now saw a chance to get himself out of prison.

"Remember me when it shall be well with thee," he said to the chief butler, "and shew kindness, I pray thee, unto me, and make mention of me unto Pharaoh, and bring me out of this house: for indeed I was stolen away out of the land of the Hebrews: and here also have I done nothing that they should put me into the dungeon."

Gladly the butler promised to remember him. Then the chief baker told his dream, hoping that Joseph would be able to give him good news also. He said that in his dream he had three white baskets on his head. In the top one were all kinds

55

of cookies such as Pharaoh liked, and the birds came and ate them all up.

Joseph at once saw the meaning of this dream, but he didn't like to tell it.

"The three baskets," he said, "are three days: yet within three days shall Pharaoh lift up thy head from off thee, and shall hang thee on a tree; and the birds shall eat thy flesh from off thee."

Poor chief baker! There were no smiles on his face now.

"And it came to pass the third day, which was Pharaoh's birthday, that he made a feast unto all his servants: and he lifted up the head of the chief butler and of the chief baker among his servants. And he restored the chief butler unto his butlership again; . . . but he hanged the chief baker"—just exactly as Joseph had told them.

Down in the prison the news soon got around as to what had happened to the chief butler and the chief baker, and Joseph must have marveled how exactly his interpretations of the two dreams had come true. No doubt, too, he kept wondering and wondering if the chief butler would mention him to Pharaoh and have him set free. But month after month passed, and no word came. The chief butler had forgotten all about him!

Poor Joseph! He had to stay in that prison another two whole years.

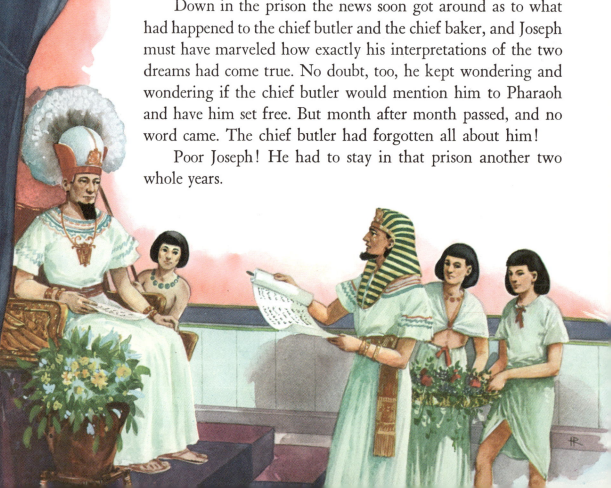

STORY 10

From the Dungeon to the Throne

ONE DAY as Joseph was going about his duties in the prison, a messenger came hurrying from the court. "Pharaoh wants to see you at once," he said.

"Me! What for?" I can hear Joseph saying.

"Come at once," repeated the messenger.

How excited Joseph must have felt at that moment! As quickly as he could "he shaved himself, and changed his raiment, and came in unto Pharaoh."

All the way from the prison to the palace he must have asked himself, "What does this mean? Why has he called for me? What have I done wrong now?"

It never occurred to him that the chief butler might have remembered him at last. But that is exactly what had happened.

Only last night Pharaoh had had a strange dream, which had worried him. He had felt sure it had an important meaning, but he could not think what it might be. So in the morning he had "called for all the magicians of Egypt, and all the wise men thereof," but none of them had been able to interpret the dream.

It was just then that the chief butler had seen a chance to get a little glory for himself by mentioning Joseph. While the magicians and the wise men were standing around trying to think up some explanation of Pharaoh's dream, he had told the king of what had happened to him in the prison two years before, and how Joseph's interpretation of his dream, and the chief baker's dream, had turned out exactly right.

Pharaoh had been interested, and, anxious to have his own dream explained, had sent for Joseph.

Now the great door into the spacious throne room opened, and Joseph was led in. Pharaoh was seated on his golden throne with gorgeously dressed officers and other servants about him. It was a marvelous sight to Joseph after all the years he had spent in the drab and dirty prison.

Bowing low to Pharaoh, he waited respectfully to find out why he had been summoned so suddenly.

"I have dreamed a dream," said Pharaoh, "and there is none that can interpret it: and I have heard say of thee, that thou canst understand a dream to interpret it."

"It is not in me," said Joseph humbly, "God shall give Pharaoh an answer of peace."

Then Pharaoh told him about two dreams he had had. One was about seven lean cows that ate up seven fat cows; and another about seven withered ears of corn that ate up seven good ears.

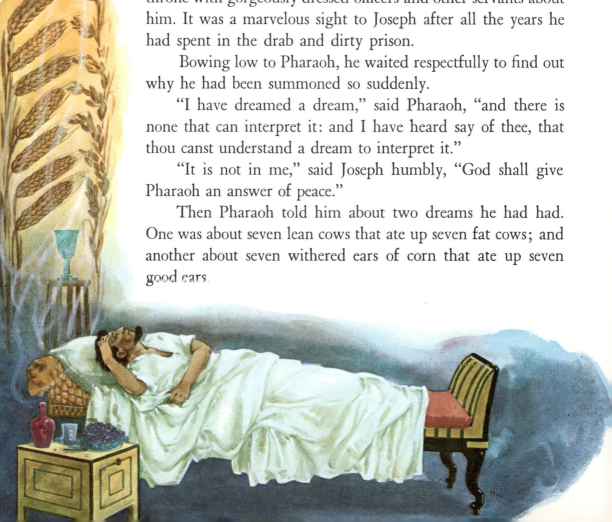

Joseph understood at once, and in a few words he told Pharaoh just what the dreams meant. Both dreams, he said, had the same meaning and were sent by God to warn Pharaoh of the coming of a great famine. There would be seven years of plenty, with wonderful harvests and lots of grain and other foodstuff; but afterward there would be seven years of the worst famine Egypt had ever seen.

"Now therefore," said Joseph, "let Pharaoh look out a man discreet and wise, and set him over the land of Egypt. . . . And let him appoint officers over the land. . . . And let them gather all the food of those good years that come, and lay up corn under the hand of Pharaoh, and let them keep food in the cities. And that food shall be for store to the land against the seven years of famine."

Pharaoh was greatly impressed, not only by the interpretation of his dream, but by this sound advice from the fine young man before him. Turning to his counselors, he said, "Can we find such a one as this is, a man in whom the Spirit of God is?"

So Joseph was chosen to be ruler over all the land of Egypt. "Only in the throne," said Pharaoh, "will I be greater than thou."

"And Pharaoh took off his ring from his hand, and put it upon Joseph's hand, and arrayed him in vestures of fine linen, and put a gold chain about his neck; and he made him to ride in the second chariot which he had; and they cried before him, Bow the knee."

If only his brothers could have seen him now! They had sold him as a slave, thinking to hurt and humble him; and here he was riding through Egypt's cities in the royal chariot, with everybody bowing before him!

Thus does God work for those who love and trust Him, defeating the plans of their enemies and making everything come out right in the end.

Should you ever find yourself in a dungeon of some sort, never fear. Be faithful, be true. For somewhere beyond is a palace and a throne, and God will lead you there.

STORY 11

Noblest of All

≈≈≈≈≈

T HE NEXT few years were very happy ones for Joseph. It must have seemed to him as though he had come out of a long, dark tunnel into a world of sunshine.

Not only did Pharaoh give him a lovely home, a splendid chariot, and a beautiful wife, but the people of Egypt loved him. They thought he was the most wonderful governor they had ever had. Never had they been so well off. For seven years in succession they had the greatest harvests they could remember. "The earth brought forth by handfuls."

When the government collected one fifth of all crops nobody grumbled, for all had so much they didn't know what to do with it. And none had a care for the future. Only Joseph knew what was coming, and he drove all over the country in his chariot arranging for the storage of the grain. In every city he built storehouses and filled them to the bursting point.

At first he tried to count all the bushels of grain that were brought in, but finally gave up. There was too much. "And

Joseph gathered corn as the sand of the sea, very much, until he left numbering; for it was without number."

Then suddenly the seven good years ended. In the eighth year, when the time came to reap the fields, there was almost no crop at all. Everything was dried up. The seven years of famine had begun.

All over the earth harvests failed, and soon millions of people were facing starvation. "And all countries came into Egypt to Joseph for to buy corn; because that the famine was so sore in all lands."

Joseph held on to his stores of grain as long as he could, for he knew they must last for many years. But finally conditions became so bad that he decided to open his storehouses and sell the corn to the hungry people. How glad they were then that he had been so wise and careful!

Up in Canaan, Jacob was beginning to get worried over the famine. In all his long life he had never seen anything like this. There was no grass for his cattle and no grain to make bread for his large family. His harvest too had failed, and now his supplies of food were getting dangerously low.

At last he called his sons together and said to them, "Behold, I have heard that there is corn in Egypt: get you down thither, and buy for us from thence; that we may live, and not die."

So ten of his sons set out for Egypt, leaving only Benjamin behind with his father.

They followed the same trail that Joseph had traveled twenty-two years before, when they sold him as a slave to the

Ishmaelites. Many times they must have thought about the
wrong they did him then, and wondered if they might meet
him in Egypt, if indeed he were still alive. But one thing they
did not expect—and that was to find him the chief man in
Egypt next to Pharaoh.

On arriving in Egypt, they inquired where they could buy
grain, and were told they must first obtain permission from the
governor. So they went to see him and bowed low before him,
never supposing for a moment that this fine big man, dressed
in the splendid robes of a high Egyptian official, and speaking
the Egyptian language, was their own brother.

But Joseph recognized them all right. He was glad to see
them too; but before letting them know who he was, he decided
to find out if they had changed at all during the years since
they had sold him into slavery.

So he put on a harsh voice and accused them of being spies.
This frightened them badly, and very humbly they replied that
they were not spies, but merely sons of an old man in the land
of Canaan. All they wanted was food, they said. But Joseph
kept on saying, "Ye are spies!"

Finally he put them in prison for three days. Perhaps this was to let them see what a prison was like, or just to give himself time to think what to do next. What he wanted most was to see his younger brother again, his own dear Benjamin; but how could this be brought about?

Finally he thought of a plan, and sent for his brothers. Then he suggested that one of them should remain in prison while the rest took what corn they needed, returned home, and came again with Benjamin. They agreed, and Joseph chose Simeon to be the hostage. As soldiers bound him, the others looked on, trembling.

Then a strange thing happened. Suddenly it came over the brothers that all this trouble had come to them because of the way they had treated Joseph long ago, and they began to say one to another: "We are verily guilty concerning our brother, in that we saw the anguish of his soul, when he besought us, and we would not hear; therefore is this distress come upon us. And Reuben answered them, saying, Spake I not unto you, saying, Do not sin against the child; and ye would not hear?"

Though they did not know it, Joseph understood every word they said; and he was so moved by their sorrow for what they had done to him that "he turned himself about from them, and wept." Dear, tenderhearted Joseph!

On their way home the brothers found all the money they

had paid for the corn inside their sacks. They couldn't understand how it could have got there, and it made them more afraid than before to return to Egypt. They did not know that Joseph, out of his love for them, had himself ordered that their money should be returned to them.

When they arrived home they told Jacob all that had happened, and how the governor of Egypt had said that they could have no more corn unless they took their youngest brother back with them.

"Benjamin!" cried Jacob. "Never!" "Joseph is not, and Simeon is not, and ye will take Benjamin away: all these things are against me."

Again and again Jacob refused to let Benjamin go to Egypt, but at last, when all their food was gone, he had to give in.

"Take also your brother," he said sadly, "and arise, go . . . : and God Almighty give you mercy before the man, that he may send away your other brother, and Benjamin. If I be bereaved of my children, I am bereaved."

So they set out again, taking double the money with them, besides a gift for the governor—and Benjamin.

Joseph was expecting them. He knew they would have to return for more food, and when word reached him that they were in the city, he decided to give them the surprise of their lives. He sent them an invitation to dine at his house.

They couldn't believe their ears. Dine with the governor! They were more frightened than ever. "It's because of the money that was in our sacks," they said to one another. "Now he is going to punish us and take us for bondmen."

But they were mistaken. When they appeared before Joseph, he began to talk to them about their father.

"Is your father well," he asked, "the old man of whom ye spake? Is he yet alive?"

"Thy servant our father is in good health," they replied, again bowing low before him.

Suddenly Joseph caught sight of Benjamin, and was so overcome at seeing his little brother again that he hurried out of the room and burst into tears. How he longed to throw his arms around him! But he dared not do it yet.

Presently Joseph returned to the dining hall, seemingly quite calm, and ordered the meal to be served. He sat alone, apart from his Egyptian officers, while his brothers, being Hebrews, sat at another table, looking in amazement at the magnificent meal that had been prepared for them. The Bible says they "marvelled one at another," and the more so when they saw how, by the governor's order, Benjamin's plate was heaped with five times as much food as anyone else's.

Yet still they did not guess who the governor was.

Then Joseph played one more trick on them. He gave orders that when their sacks were filled with grain this time, his own silver cup was to be placed in Benjamin's sack.

Presently the brothers set off for home, very proud of themselves at having been invited to dinner with the governor of Egypt and very happy that everything had turned out so well after all. But soon they heard the sound of horses galloping, and, looking round, were horrified to find that it was the governor's steward, with a bodyguard, coming to arrest them!

66

Roughly the steward accused them of stealing the governor's silver cup, which he greatly prized.

Of course they denied doing any such thing, and their blank looks were enough to convince anybody that they were innocent. But the steward demanded that the sacks be examined, and of course, the cup was found in Benjamin's sack.

What a sad journey that was back to the city! All their joy of the morning was gone. Now they were filled with new fears.

Back at the governor's palace, they once more fell on their faces before Joseph, pleading their innocence. This was more than Joseph could stand. Suddenly he raised his voice in command, saying, "Cause every man to go out from me!"

"And there stood no man with him, while Joseph made himself known unto his brethren."

What a meeting was that!

"And he wept aloud: and the Egyptians and the house of Pharaoh heard."

At first the brothers wondered what all this might mean. Then, as Joseph was able to control himself, he said, "I am Joseph; doth my father yet live?"

Then they were afraid. Joseph! Could this be Joseph? If it were, what would he do to them in revenge for all they had made him suffer?

But there was no revenge in Joseph's heart. Only love. He had forgiven them long ago, and all he wanted was to be friends again.

In their fear they had moved away from him, but he said, so gently, "Come near to me, I pray you."

"And they came near. And he said, I am Joseph your brother, whom ye sold into Egypt. Now therefore be not grieved, nor angry with yourselves, that ye sold me hither: for God did send me before you to preserve life. For these two years hath the famine been in the land: and yet there are five years, in which there shall neither be earing nor harvest. And God sent me before you to preserve you a posterity in the earth, and to save your lives by a great deliverance. So now it was not you that sent me hither, but God."

How beautifully did he try to take all the worry out of their hearts! He didn't want them to blame themselves for what happened; all was in the providence of God.

Only a truly noble man could speak like that!

Then he told them of his plan to bring the whole family into the land of Goshen, a section of Egypt, where he could provide them with food through the five years of famine still to come.

"There will I nourish thee," he said, "lest thou, and thy household, and all that thou hast, come to poverty."

There was not a trace of meanness in Joseph's character. Powerful and wealthy though he was, he never once thought of trying to get even with these men who had been so cruel to him.

"And he fell upon his brother Benjamin's neck, and wept; and Benjamin wept upon his neck. Moreover he kissed all his brethren, and wept upon them."

Yes, he kissed them all. Reuben, Simeon, Judah—every one, even those who had actually thrown him into the pit, and sold him into slavery. He kissed them! What love! What forgiveness! Surely he was indeed the noblest of them all. How God must have loved him for his greatness of spirit!

"And the fame thereof was heard in Pharaoh's house" as the news passed from one to another, "Joseph's brethren are come!"

Pharaoh was pleased at what had happened, and told Joseph to feel free to invite all his family to come and live in Egypt.

"Take your father and your households, and come unto me," he said in a generous mood, "and I will give you the good of the land of Egypt." He also ordered that wagons should be provided so that the women and children and Joseph's old father could travel in comfort.

As a parting gift Joseph gave to each of his brothers "changes of raiment," meaning new clothes to wear, and to Benjamin "three hundred pieces of silver, and five changes of raiment." To his father he sent "ten asses laden with the good things of Egypt, and ten she asses laden with corn and bread and meat for his father by the way." He tried to think of everything that would make them happy and at ease. Then with a smile, remembering their old weakness, he said to them as they left, "See that ye fall not out by the way."

When the brothers reached home they all trooped into their old father's tent crying, "Joseph is yet alive, and he is governor over all the land of Egypt."

Jacob would not believe them. It didn't seem possible. Why, the dear boy had been dead more than twenty years.

"He isn't dead," they kept on saying. "He's alive. We saw him and talked with him." And then they told him what had happened, and all that Joseph had said to them. Still the old man would not believe them.

Then they took him outside and showed him the wagons loaded with good things which only Joseph's loving heart could have provided. Then he knew the story must be true. A smile came over his face, and a new light shone in his eyes. "It is enough!" he cried. "Joseph my son is yet alive: I will go and see him before I die."

No time was lost in getting everything ready for the journey, for Jacob now had but one idea in mind—to see his precious Joseph again.

As the caravan paused en route at Beersheba, Jacob offered up sacrifices of joy and thanksgiving to God. And that night God spoke to him, saying, "Jacob, Jacob." And he said, "Here am I."

And God said, "I am God, the God of thy father: fear not to go down into Egypt; . . . and I will also surely bring thee up again: and Joseph shall put his hand upon thine eyes."

Cheered by this kindly message, Jacob went on his way with new courage, "and the sons of Israel carried Jacob their father, and their little ones, and their wives, in the wagons which Pharaoh had sent to carry him.

"And they took their cattle, and their goods, which they had gotten in the land of Canaan, and came into Egypt."

How happy and excited Joseph must have been when news reached him that his father was nearing Egypt! The Bible tells us that "he made ready his chariot, and went up to meet Israel his father, to Goshen, and presented himself unto him; and he fell on his neck, and wept on his neck a good while.

"And Israel said unto Joseph, Now let me die, since I have seen thy face, because thou art yet alive."

But he didn't die, not then. He was so happy to see Joseph again he lived another seventeen years!

"And Israel dwelt in the land of Egypt, in the country of Goshen; and they had possessions therein, and grew, and multiplied exceedingly."

Thus through the faithfulness and loyalty of one noble, godly boy, thousands of people were saved from starvation, the "seed of the woman" was once more preserved, and the name of the God of heaven, the God of Joseph, and the God of Israel was made known in all the world.

PART II

Stories of Israel in Egypt

(Exodus 1:1-10:29)

≈≈≈≈≈

STORY 1

Light in the Darkness

≈≈≈≈≈≈≈≈≈≈≈≈≈≈≈≈≈≈≈≈

GRANDPA, shall we ever see the beautiful land you keep telling us about?"

"Someday," said Joseph, "some happy day."

The slave boy who became governor of Egypt was now more than a hundred years old. A grandfather of Ephraim's children "of the third generation," he was also the great-uncle of a host of boys and girls belonging to the families of his eleven brothers.

I can see these children running into his palace to talk to him, for his kind, gentle heart made him beloved of all. And what wonderful stories he had to tell them! How they loved to hear him speak of the old days when he was a boy in Canaan, especially as he pictured the green hills, the snow-capped mountains, and the rushing waterfalls of his homeland! For Canaan was their homeland too, though they had never seen it, and could only dream about it.

75

← PAINTING BY HERBERT RUDEEN © BY REVIEW AND HERALD

God's people, who had moved to Egypt, built homes there and were very happy during the life of Joseph, for God had prospered him and made him a wise ruler under Pharaoh.

He longed to go back there, but never could. There was never time. He was always too busy. His many duties made it impossible. And then he became too old to go.

At last there came a day when he felt that death was near. Calling his brothers to him for the last time, he said to them, "I die: and God will surely visit you, and bring you out of this land unto the land which he sware to Abraham, to Isaac, and to Jacob. . . . And ye shall carry up my bones from hence."

He knew that it was not God's plan for them to live always in the midst of a heathen nation. Someday, somehow, He would lead them back to the beautiful land from which they had come. And he wanted to go along too. That is why he said, "Carry up my bones." If he could not go to Canaan in life, at least he would rest there in death.

The brothers promised to remember his dying wish, and Joseph, contented, breathed his last.

We are not told anything about his funeral, but it must have been a very splendid one. No doubt there was a great procession, with thousands of people following the body of the kind, wise governor to its resting place.

His tomb may well have been near the pyramids, where so many of the great men of Egypt were buried; and for years passers-by would say, "There lies one of the finest leaders this country ever knew."

In the course of time, however, "there arose up a new king over Egypt, which knew not Joseph."

This new king not only did not remember Joseph; he knew little, if anything, about how or why the children of Israel came to be living in Egypt. All he knew was that there were now more Israelites than Egyptians in the country, and he didn't like it. Nor did his fellow Egyptians like it. They grumbled about the Israelites' owning the finest land and holding important positions in the government.

As one complaint after another was made, Pharaoh decided that something must be done. So, calling his counselors together, he said to them, "Behold, the people of the children of Israel are more and mightier than we: come on, let us deal wisely with them; lest they multiply, and it come to pass, that, when there falleth out any war, they join also unto our enemies, and fight against us, and so get them up out of the land."

The counselors needed no urging to deal with the Hebrews. They had been waiting for the chance. Now they worked out a plan to get the better of them. It was hard and cruel. No longer would the Hebrews be treated as equals, but as slaves. No longer would they be allowed to work for themselves or for their own profit; from now on they would have to labor for the state.

Imagine how the children of Israel must have felt as news of the king's decree spread among them! I can almost hear them saying, "It's slavery! They have made us slaves!"

That is exactly what had happened. Suddenly they real-

ized that the good old days under Joseph's kindly rule had gone forever. Now they were told what to do, and were kicked and beaten if they failed to obey. The Egyptians "set over them taskmasters to afflict them with their burdens. And they built for Pharaoh treasure cities, Pithom and Raamses."

Day after day they toiled in the blazing heat. From sunrise to sunset men, women, and children made bricks, mixed mortar, and built walls, while the taskmasters stood by, whips in their hands, ready to punish anyone who should try to rest.

But though the Egyptians made the lives of the Hebrews "bitter with hard bondage," they did not succeed in breaking their spirit. Though the Israelites were often sad and discouraged, hope never left their hearts. And the more Pharaoh afflicted them, "the more they multiplied and grew."

Back in their homes at night they would talk about God's promise to Abraham, which had been handed down from father to son for many, many years: "Know of a surety that thy seed shall be a stranger in a land that is not their's, and shall serve them; and they shall afflict them four hundred years. . . . But in the fourth generation they shall come hither again."

Again and again they must have tried to figure out when the time would be up, and which was the "fourth generation." Often they must have cried in their sorrow, "How long, O Lord, how long?"

Then someone would pass by Joseph's tomb and remember his promise: "God will surely visit you, and bring you out of this land." And once more light would break through the darkness, hope would rise, and hearts would be brave again.

STORY 2

Baby to the Rescue

RIDING in his chariot one day to inspect his two new treasure cities, Pithom and Raamses, Pharaoh saw something that made him first worried, then angry.

It seemed to him that he had never seen so many Hebrews in all his life. They were in the fields and about the brickkilns. They were unloading blocks of stone from barges on the river and hauling other blocks into place on the houses and temples they were building. They were everywhere.

The worst of it was that they all looked so strong and healthy. He had thought to kill them off with hard work, but here they were more numerous than ever. His plans had gone wrong.

Pharaoh decided that there was only one thing to do. If he could not get rid of the Hebrews by working them to death, he would reduce their numbers some other way. And what could be easier than killing their children as soon as they were born?

So he made a decree that every baby boy must be thrown into the river.

As the Hebrew fathers and mothers heard the dreadful news their faces turned pale. At first they could hardly believe it. Surely no ruler could be so cruel as to order that all baby boys should be murdered like this.

But it *was* true, and soon terror filled all hearts as stories were told of soldiers taking babies away from their mothers and flinging them into the Nile to drown or be eaten by crocodiles. Imagine how the people must have felt in homes where a baby was on the way, or had just arrived! Imagine how the older brothers and sisters must have worried themselves sick, let alone the fathers and mothers.

This was Israel's darkest hour. They had put up with the long hours of toil and the merciless deeds of the taskmasters, but this cold-blooded killing of their children was too much to bear. It made them want to leave Egypt as they had never wanted to leave it before. They began to pray for deliverance as they had never prayed before. They wanted help *now*.

At this very moment, when things seemed as though they couldn't get worse, when everybody was on the verge of despair, God sent a baby to the rescue.

It happened this way: One day a baby boy turned up in the home of Amram and Jochebed. These godly Hebrews had a little girl called Miriam and a little boy named Aaron, and they had wanted another little boy so much. But now! Oh, dear! Suppose the soldiers should find him!

Nobody knows for sure what name the parents gave this

new baby. Maybe it was Abraham, or Enoch, or Joseph. If so, it got lost. Later on, as we shall see, he was given another name, and this one stuck to him for life.

Jochebed was a devoted mother, and she made up her mind that the soldiers wouldn't get her baby, not if she could help it. Somehow or other she managed to keep him hidden for three months. But it is pretty hard to hide a three-month-old baby anywhere. Just think of the noise he makes when he cries!

One day, when Jochebed knew she couldn't keep her secret any longer, she got a bright idea. She would make a little boat, put the baby in it, and set it afloat near the bank of the river. Perhaps, who could tell?—some kindhearted Egyptian woman passing by might find it and take pity on the poor little thing inside. It seemed to be the only way out, the desperate chance, and she decided to take it. It was better than doing nothing. Any moment the soldiers might burst into the house and snatch her baby away.

So she wove a basket with reeds from the river, making it watertight by coating it with mud and pitch. When the pitch was dry she fixed a soft little bed inside and tenderly—oh, so

tenderly!—laid her baby in it. Then she kissed him good-by, closed the lid, and carried the basket to the riverbank. Here, with a breaking heart and tears running down her cheeks, she placed it gently among the bulrushes. Then she went home to ask God to protect her child, leaving Miriam to watch what would happen.

Miriam was not alone on that riverbank. Angels were there, too, watching with her. For this was a very special baby for whom God had planned a very wonderful future.

After awhile who should walk by but Pharaoh's daughter, attended by some of her maids. Suddenly she caught sight of the strange oblong basket in the bulrushes, and sent one of her maids to fetch it. Lifting the lid, she saw a beautiful baby boy inside, and the poor little thing was crying.

"This is one of the Hebrews' children," she said. Perhaps she picked him up and loved him. The Bible says she "had compassion on him," and that means a lot. At least she wasn't cruel and hardhearted like her father.

BABY TO THE RESCUE

As her maids crowded round to look at the baby, wondering what to do with him, Miriam came sidling up. It must have taken a lot of courage for her to speak to the princess, but with her baby brother's life at stake she was ready to dare anything.

"Please, ma'am," she said, "shall I go and call to thee a nurse of the Hebrew women, that she may nurse the child for thee?"

Pharaoh's daughter was relieved. This seemed to be a good way out of a very awkward situation. "Go," she said, and Miriam ran like the wind to find her mother.

"Mother, Mother!" I can hear her gasping as she rushed into the house. "Come quickly, come quickly! The princess has found baby brother!"

And how long do you suppose it took Jochebed to get from her house to the riverbank? Not very long. Never had she run so fast in her life. And there were the princess and her maids and the baby crying for his dinner. She was so happy

she didn't know whether to laugh or to cry, but she tried to keep a straight face so the princess wouldn't think that she was the child's mother.

Then the princess spoke to her, and she could hardly believe her ears. "Take this child away," she said gently, "and nurse it for me, and I will give thee thy wages."

The way Jochebed took the baby and cuddled it was enough to give her away, but if the princess guessed the truth, she didn't say anything. As she left with her maids for the palace, Jochebed and Miriam hurried happily homeward, their hearts overflowing with thankfulness to God for the way He had spared their precious little boy.

It was all too wonderful to believe. Not only did they have their baby back, but the soldiers could never kill him now. He was a ward of the princess, and she was going to pay his mother wages for his keep! She could give him the best food, the best of care, and Pharaoh's daughter would pay for it!

Oh, yes, the baby had a new name now. The princess had given it to him down there by the river. Moses, she said it was to be—Moses, meaning "drawn out," because, she said, "I drew him out of the water."

If she had known who this child would be someday, and what he would do, would she have saved his life? I don't know. Perhaps she would. For this baby was the very one whom God had sent to rescue His people and lead them out of Egypt to freedom.

≈≈≈≈≈≈≈≈≈

STORY 3

Training a Prince

≈≈≈≈≈≈≈≈≈≈≈≈≈≈≈≈≈≈≈≈

AS JOCHEBED thought over what had happened down there by the river, it slowly dawned upon her that, though she had her baby back safe and sound, he didn't really belong to her any more. This boy with the new name had a new mother. Someday the princess would send for him and take him away, and never give him back again. He would grow up to be not *her* child, not "one of the Hebrews' children," but a prince of Egypt.

"How long shall I be able to keep him?" she must have asked herself over and over again. One year, two years, ten years? She could not tell. But she made up her mind that during the time she was allowed to keep him, whether long or short, she would give him the best training possible.

Knowing that in the palace he would meet many evil temptations, she sought to anchor his little heart to God. She taught him to pray and to sing little songs of praise. Over and over again she told him the story of creation and the Fall, and

85

of God's plan of salvation—that sweet and beautiful story that had been handed down from father to son from the days of Adam and Eve.

God, she taught him, is a holy God, who expects all His children to be good and pure and true. Those who want His blessing must follow His teachings and obey His laws.

She told him also about the history of his people and how Abraham had promised that someday they would all be delivered from bondage and taken back to Canaan.

Then, too, she told him of his own wonderful deliverance from death, and of her conviction that, if he kept loyal and true to God, a great destiny lay ahead of him.

All too quickly the years went by. Then one day, when Moses was twelve years old, the fateful message arrived. The princess wanted her son. He was to be brought to the palace at once.

What a sad day was that! Mother choking back her sobs as she packed up the few things he would need to take along with him. Father trying hard to hide his grief. Miriam weeping her heart out. Aaron looking glum, not sure whether to be sad or envious.

Perhaps some soldiers came in a chariot to fetch him. I don't know. Perhaps just Jochebed and Moses walked to the palace together. Somehow I seem to see them there outside the palace gates, just before they swung open, the boy's heart full of questioning, the mother's full of fears and sadness.

TRAINING A PRINCE

Then came the last good-bys, the last promises to remember, the last assurances of undying love.

As the guards took Moses inside, and the gates closed behind him, the great palace must have seemed a very lonely place to him. No doubt his new mother tried to be specially kind to him, but somehow it wasn't the same. Probably he cried himself to sleep that night, thinking that he was forever separated from his home and dear ones, and could never return to them.

But with the morning came new interests. Everywhere he turned there were wonderful things to see. Life here was so different from all he had known in the humble little cottage that had been his home till now.

Being a lad of fine appearance, "exceeding fair" as the Bible tells us, he was soon a favorite in the court. Everybody loved him. The best teachers in the land were brought in to tutor him. He had lessons in mathematics, law, medicine, military science, and many other things until, as time went by, he became "learned in all the wisdom of the Egyptians, and was mighty in words and in deeds."

No longer a boy, Moses was now in the prime of life. Strong of body and keen of mind, he already had the makings of a great leader. He could ride a horse or drive a chariot with skill and daring. So well had he applied himself to his studies that there was little about the history, geography, and religion of Egypt that he did not know.

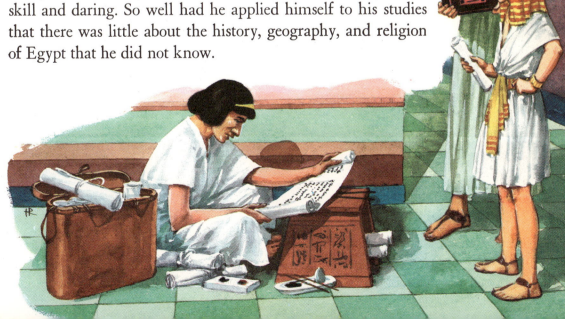

All the court—indeed, all Egypt—knew that here was a young man of unusual gifts, well able to take Pharaoh's place. And Moses himself was not unaware that he was in direct line to the throne. Someday, he knew, if he so desired, he could become ruler of Egypt.

Yet amid all his studies and all his busy life, he never forgot the things his mother had told him in his boyhood. Not a day passed but he thought of God and of what mother had said God wanted him to be and to do. As the years slipped by, he felt more and more out of place in the palace. Deep loyalties, which court life could not change, drew him toward his people, now suffering greater hardships than ever.

Reports of the terrible way the Hebrew slaves were being treated reached him from time to time. Sometimes he wondered whether he should go to their aid. He counted the cost of revealing that he was not an Egyptian after all, but belonged to the very people whom the Egyptians despised. He knew he would lose his position and his chance for the throne. What should he do?

When he said his prayers he talked with God about it all, asking Him for guidance. Then one night he made his decision—"choosing rather to suffer affliction with the people of God, than to enjoy the pleasures of sin for a season; esteeming the reproach of Christ greater riches than the treasures in Egypt."

It was a great and noble choice to make, and proved to be a turning point in the history of Israel and of the world.

STORY 4

Flight for Life

AS A PRINCE of Egypt and the pride and joy of his royal mother, Moses had everything a young man could wish. Lots of money, a beautiful home, many servants, chariots, and horses—all were his.

Because of his position people made a fuss over him, flattered him, and ran to do whatever he asked them. It was enough to turn any boy's head, and it would have been surprising if he did not have a pretty high opinion of himself and of what he could do.

As he thought about the suffering of his people, he planned one scheme after another to bring about their deliverance. Perhaps this would work, or that. But he had one great lesson to learn: the deliverance, when it came, would not be wrought by him, but by God.

No one in the court had any idea what was going on in his mind. No one doubted his loyalty to Pharaoh. All would have been shocked had they known that he had decided to

89

take the part of the Hebrew slaves and try to bring their bondage to an end. So, of course, nobody took any notice when one day he left the palace, mounted his chariot, and rode out to a section of the country where the Hebrews were working. People bowed to him and smiled at him, just as they always did when they saw this handsome young prince.

Leaving the city behind him, he found himself at length on a lonely, deserted stretch of road. Then it was that he came upon a sight that sickened him. One of the Egyptian taskmasters was cruelly beating a Hebrew slave. Looking this way and that to make sure that no one was looking, Moses leaped from his chariot, strode over to the bully, and with one blow felled him to the ground.

The poor Hebrew, astonished to see a prince of the royal house striking down one of the king's taskmasters, ran as fast as he could to tell the news to his people. Meanwhile Moses was left with the body of the man he had killed. Not wanting the Hebrews—or himself—to be accused of murdering an officer, he decided to bury him in the sand.

Returning to the palace, he felt rather pleased with himself. He had made a good start. He felt sure that when the Hebrews heard of what he had done—as they surely would—they would rejoice that they had a friend at court who was willing to help them. He never dreamed they would betray him. "For he supposed his brethren would have understood how that God by his hand would deliver them: but they understood not."

Confident that all was going well, he went out again the next day to see what he could do for his people. This time

91

Although Moses was the adopted son of Pharoh's daughter, he loved his own people, and because he could not stand to see them abused, e forsook the royal courts to go into exile.

he came across two Hebrews struggling together, with the stronger one beating the other mercilessly. Moses was surprised and disappointed. How could he help his people if they fought among themselves? "Sirs," he called to them, "ye are brethren; why do ye wrong one to another?"

He hoped they would make friends and thank him for his good advice; but instead, as he tried to separate them, the man who was chiefly at fault turned on him and said, "Who made thee a ruler and a judge over us? wilt thou kill me, as thou diddest the Egyptian yesterday?"

Moses was shocked. So his action of yesterday was known! He had buried the body, but not the deed. If this unfriendly Hebrew knew of it, all Egypt must know too. Perhaps even Pharaoh had heard.

Anxiously he hurried back to the palace. Here he found that his worst fears were true. Everybody was talking about him and what he had done. His secret was on everybody's lips. Somehow the news had been flashed all over the country that Prince Moses had killed one of the king's officers for beating a Hebrew slave!

Pharaoh, he learned, was very angry. Such a deed was unpardonable. It must be punished by death. An order had already gone out for his arrest and execution.

92

How he escaped we do not know. No doubt some of his friends helped him. Perhaps the princess used her power on his behalf. Somehow he managed to get away without being caught.

The safest place to go, he thought, was the land of Midian. Here nobody would know him, and he could hide till this whole sorry affair had been forgotten.

But it must have been with a very heavy heart that he started out on his journey. As he bade farewell to Egypt and saw the pyramids gradually fading out of sight behind him, he knew that life would never be the same again. Gone forever were the easy days in the palace. From now on he would know the sorrow and hardship of a homeless exile.

Hardest to bear was the thought of the foolish mistake he had made. He should never have killed that Egyptian. He had acted rashly. He should have taken more time to work out his plans. He had spoiled his chance to help his people. Now who could deliver them?

Day after day he dragged his weary feet over the hot, dry sand of the desert. Night after night he slept in the open, his eyes wet with tears at the thought of the mess he had made.

At last he came into Midian and sat down by a well. As evening drew on he saw seven young girls coming toward him. After the loneliness of the desert they must have been a very welcome sight.

He learned that they were sisters, daughters of Jethro, an important man in those parts. Presently, as they began to draw water from the well for the sheep they had with them, some rough shepherds arrived and tried to drive them away. This was too much for Moses, who had been trained in courtesy at home and in the court. Gallantly he stood up for the girls, and told the shepherds to behave themselves. Then he drew water from the well himself, and poured it into the troughs for the sheep to drink. This was a strange thing for a prince of Egypt to do, but it was the first happy moment he had had in many a long day.

When the sheep were watered, the seven girls bade him good-by and hurried home. When they arrived their father asked them why they were back so much earlier than usual. They said it was because an Egyptian had befriended them against the shepherds, and had watered the flock. "Then where is he?" asked Jethro. "Why did you leave him at the well? Go and bring him home to supper."

So the seven girls came trooping back to the well and apologized to Moses for having seemed so ungracious. Then they took him back home with them. And there he stayed for many years, until he had learned the lesson God wanted to teach him.

Strangely enough, it took exactly as long for him to learn this lesson from the wisdom of God as it had taken him to become "learned in all the wisdom of the Egyptians."

STORY 5

Voice in the Desert

YEAR after year went by. Moses married Zipporah, one of those seven girls whom he had met at the well. They had two children. The first he called Gershom, meaning "a stranger here," because he had been "a stranger in a strange land." The second he called Eliezer, meaning "my God is an help"—a very lovely thought behind a boy's name.

One day a messenger arrived to say that the Pharaoh who had threatened to kill Moses was dead. This was good news, but the rest was bad. Things were no better for the children of Israel. Their bondage was as cruel as ever.

If Moses wondered whether he should now return to Egypt and try to help his people, he dismissed the idea at once. "How can I help them now?" he asked himself. "I have no power or influence any more. Everybody has forgotten me. If I were to go back now, they wouldn't even recognize me."

Thus, little by little, he had come to the place where he was ready to admit that *he* could not deliver Israel. Years ago

95

he had thought maybe he could. Now he knew he couldn't. And it was when he had reached this place that God was ready and able to use him.

Eighty years had passed since he had been found by the princess in the little basket in the bulrushes. The first forty years he had spent in Egypt learning the wisdom of the Egyptians. The last forty he had spent as a shepherd in Midian, unlearning much that he had learned before.

No longer the proud young prince, he was old and tired and perhaps a little sad. But he need not have been discouraged, for God had not left him. Every hour of every day since he was born God had watched over him. Yes, and God still remembered Jochebed's prayers for him and his own resolve to do the right at all costs. Though Moses did not realize it, God was still counting on him to be the champion of His people and bring them out of bondage into freedom.

Now the time had come. God was ready, and His man was ready. And they met, not in a palace, not beside one of the pyramids, but by a bush in the desert.

Wandering over the barren hills one day, Moses suddenly noticed a strange sight. A bush seemed to be on fire. Yet it did not burn away. He could not explain it, and said to himself, "I will now turn aside, and see this great sight, why the bush is not burnt." In all the years he had studied science in Egypt he had never heard of anything like this.

Then a voice called his name, "Moses, Moses." He looked around. There was nobody he could see. He had thought he was alone in the wilderness. But he was not alone. Somebody

2-7

While tending sheep, Moses was startled to see a bush all afire yet not burning up. When he drew nearer, God spoke to him out of the flames and told him to lead Israel out of Egypt.

was there, very close to him, somebody who knew his name.

Then the voice spoke again. "Don't come any nearer; take off your shoes, for the place where you are standing is holy ground."

Now Moses knew that God had come to speak to him. Quickly he removed his shoes and bowed his head. Up to this moment he had been anxious to examine the burning bush. Now "he was afraid to look upon God."

And God said: "I am the God of thy father, the God of Abraham, the God of Isaac, and the God of Jacob. . . . I have surely seen the affliction of my people which are in Egypt, and have heard their cry by reason of their taskmasters; for I know their sorrows; and I am come down to deliver them."

As Moses listened, his heart was touched by God's compassion for His people. During the forty years since he had left Egypt he had almost forgotten what was going on there. But God had not forgotten. Not a sorrow, not a tear in all the long, long years, had passed unnoticed by Him.

"But why is He telling me?" Moses must have thought to himself. "Why has He come to speak to me in this wilderness?" He soon found out.

"Come now therefore," God said, "and I will send thee unto Pharaoh, that thou mayest bring forth my people the children of Israel out of Egypt."

No, he couldn't go now. There was a time when he would have been glad to, but not now. When he was younger, perhaps, but not at eighty years of age. He was too old, too weary, too much of a shepherd. "Who am I," he said, "that I should

go unto Pharaoh, and that I should bring forth the children of Israel out of Egypt?"

He had lost all of his old self-confidence. And God knew it. At last he was ready for the great task God had for him to do.

"Certainly I will be with thee," God said. "You won't be going alone. You can trust Me at all times to help you."

But Moses did not want to go. He began to make excuses. The people wouldn't believe him; they wouldn't believe that he had met God in the wilderness; he was "slow of speech," and wouldn't know what to say.

Patiently God answered all his objections, and gave him signs to convince both him and the people.

"What do you have in your hand?" God asked.

"A rod," said Moses.

"Cast it on the ground," said God.

Moses did so, and his rod became a serpent. Startled, he fled before it.

"Take it by the tail," said God.

That took courage, but Moses obeyed, and the serpent became a rod again.

Next God made Moses' hand all white with leprosy, and a moment later made it completely whole as before.

Moses was impressed, but not yet willing to go.

"O my Lord," he said, "send somebody else."

But God did not want to send somebody else. He wanted Moses. However, He agreed that Aaron should go with him to give him courage and to do the talking. "I know that he can speak well," said God. "And also, behold, he cometh forth to meet thee."

This was wonderful news. Aaron coming to meet him! Why, he hadn't seen his brother for forty years. How good it would be to see him again!

What Moses didn't know was that God had already spoken to Aaron and said, "Go into the wilderness to meet Moses."

So the two brothers were on their way, one journeying from Egypt, the other from Midian. Two brothers looking for each other in a great, wide wilderness! However could they hope to meet in such a wild, desolate country? But they did.

They met "in the mount of God."

And there they kissed each other, so glad were they to be together again.

STORY 6

God's Sevenfold Promise

WHAT a lot of things Moses and Aaron had to talk about when they met in the wilderness! They must have talked for hours. Aaron told all that had happened in Egypt since Moses fled from Pharaoh's court, and Moses told all that had happened to him from the day he arrived in Midian till he met God at the burning bush.

"And Moses told Aaron all the words of the Lord who had sent him, and all the signs which he had commanded him." As they confided in each other how God had spoken to them, they felt sure He was calling them both to do a great work for Him, and that there was nothing they could do but obey. Perhaps there on that mountainside they knelt in prayer, thanking God for the way He had led them through all the long, long years since last they had met, and asking Him to guide them through the days ahead.

At last the two old brothers, one eighty, the other eighty-three, started on their way back to Egypt—the land of bondage, tyranny, and tears. As hour after hour they walked along through the wild, desolate country, they talked of what they would do when they got there. First of all, they would meet the leading men among the Israelites and tell them what had happened at the burning bush. If these men believed their story, and what God had promised, then they would go to Pharaoh and ask him to set the people free.

And this is what they did. On reaching Egypt they arranged a meeting with the elders of Israel, and "Aaron spake all the words which the Lord had spoken unto Moses, and did the signs in the sight of the people."

As the people saw the rod become a serpent and Moses' hand become first leprous, then healthy again, they were convinced that both men were telling the truth. And when they heard that God had said, "I know their sorrows; and I am

GOD'S SEVENFOLD PROMISE

come down to deliver them," they wept for joy and "bowed their heads and worshipped."

You may be sure that it didn't take long for word to get around about what had happened at that meeting, and as the news spread from tent to tent a great new hope surged up among the poor Hebrews. God had heard their prayers! He was about to save them! Joseph's promise would soon be fulfilled!

But things didn't go too well the next day. When Moses and Aaron met Pharaoh they found it was not going to be as easy as they had thought to set Israel free. Pharaoh had no intention whatever of letting them go.

PAINTING BY HERBERT RUDEEN AFTER E. J. POYNTER

Said Aaron, "Thus saith the Lord God of Israel, Let my people go, that they may hold a feast unto me in the wilderness."

"Who is the Lord," snorted Pharaoh, "that I should obey his voice to let Israel go? I know not the Lord, neither will I let Israel go."

This was bad enough, but worse was to follow.

When Moses and Aaron explained that all they wanted at the moment was that their people might go "three days' journey into the desert, and sacrifice unto the Lord," Pharaoh was furious. Whoever heard of such a thing! Slaves asking for a whole week's vacation! Ridiculous! And if they thought they could take a week off, they were not working hard enough. They must be given more to do.

So Pharaoh decreed that from now on the people of Israel would not be given straw for their brickmaking, but would have to gather it themselves while still making the same number of bricks as before.

When the Israelites heard about this they were frightened. How could they make the same number of bricks and spend a lot of time trying to find straw? It was impossible. And when they tried to do so the taskmasters beat them without mercy, shouting, "Fulfil your works, your daily tasks, as when there was straw."

The leaders of Israel at last complained to Pharaoh, but all he said to them was, "Ye are idle, ye are idle: therefore ye say, Let us go and do sacrifice to the Lord."

Meeting Moses and Aaron, the Israelites turned on them in anger. "Look what you have done to us!" they said. "We

104

are worse off than ever. A nice way to deliver us from bondage!"

Very sad and sorry, Moses knelt in prayer to God. "Why has this happened?" he asked. "Why did you send me? 'For since I came to Pharaoh to speak in thy name, he hath done evil to this people; neither hast thou delivered thy people at all.'"

But if Moses was discouraged, God was not. He never is. He always knows what He is going to do next.

"Now shalt thou see what I will do to Pharaoh," He said: "for with a strong hand shall he let them go, and with a strong hand shall he drive them out of his land."

This was hard for Moses to believe, after all that had happened. So now God gave him a sevenfold promise, which he was to pass on to the children of Israel. Tell them, said God:

"I will bring you out from under the burdens of the Egyptians, . . . I will rid you out of their bondage, . . . I will redeem you, . . . I will take you to me for a people, . . . I will be to you a God. . . . I will bring you in unto the land, concerning the which I did swear to give it to Abraham, . . . I will give it you for an inheritance."

Seven times God said it. "I will . . . I will . . . I will."

Moses believed. But the people didn't. When he passed on the sevenfold promise to them, they refused to listen "for anguish of spirit, and for cruel bondage." Their spirits were crushed. Their hopes were dead. Things had never looked so dark to them. Yet it was the darkness before the dawn. For the hour of their deliverance was at hand.

STORY 7

Frogs in the Palace

A FEW days later Moses and Aaron went to see Pharaoh again. As soon as he saw them, he demanded that they work a miracle to prove the power of their God.

Aaron at once cast down his rod in front of Pharaoh, and it became a serpent. The king was impressed, but he was not willing to admit that this was a sign of the power of the Hebrews' God. Suspecting it was just magic, he called for his own magicians, and ordered them to do the same trick.

They did. As soon as their rods hit the floor they became serpents. Now there were several serpents crawling all over the place! For a moment it looked as though Moses and Aaron were nothing more than two smart magicians. But then a strange thing happened. Aaron's serpent went up to one of the other serpents and swallowed it. Then it went after another and another, until it had swallowed them all. When the last one had disappeared, Aaron took his serpent by the tail, and it became a rod again.

106

FROGS IN THE PALACE

It was all very mysterious. Again Pharaoh was impressed, especially as his magicians looked very silly without their rods. But he hardened his heart and refused to do what Moses and Aaron wanted.

Next day, as Pharaoh went down to the river for his morning bath, he found Moses and Aaron waiting for him on the bank. No doubt he was very much annoyed to see them again so soon and in such a place; and when Aaron began to call to him in a loud voice he must have been very angry. But he stopped and listened. What was the old man saying? They were strange words from a Hebrew slave.

"Thus saith the Lord, In this thou shalt know that I am the Lord: behold, I will smite with the rod that is in mine hand upon the waters which are in the river, and they shall be turned to blood."

"The man must be mad!" thought Pharaoh. "Does he think he can turn the waters of the Nile into blood?"

But even as he spoke a dreadful smell came from the river. Turning to see what was the matter, he noticed that the water had turned a dull red color. Dead fish were coming to the surface and being washed up on the bank at his feet. It was a dreadful sight. Sickened, he "turned and went into his house" while "all the Egyptians digged round about the river for water to drink."

Did Pharaoh let Israel go now? He did not. Instead, he called his magicians and ordered them to turn water into blood. They did. Not the Nile, of course, but enough water to con-

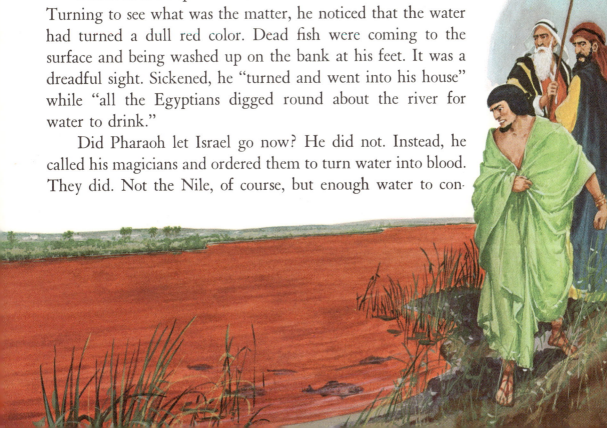

vince Pharaoh that Moses and Aaron were just using some special magic. No! he would not listen to them, nor would he let Israel go.

Then came the frogs, millions and millions of them. They swarmed all over Egypt. They jumped through the open doors and windows of the people's homes until nobody knew what to do with them. They came into Pharaoh's palace, into his bedroom, even on his bed. They got into his kitchen, into the ovens, and even into the dough that was being made into bread for him to eat.

Pharaoh simply could not get away from the frogs. He stepped on them, sat on them, slept on them. He ordered his servants to kill them, but the more they killed, the more there seemed to be. There was no end to them.

Egyptians had seen swarms of frogs before, but never a plague such as this. They began to complain to Pharaoh. But he could do nothing to help them.

At last, unable to stand it any longer, he sent for Moses and Aaron. "Ask your God to take the frogs away," he said, " 'and I will let the people go, that they may do sacrifice unto the Lord.' "

"When would you like the frogs to be gone?" asked Moses.

"To morrow!" said Pharaoh.

"Very well," said Moses. "It shall be as you say, so that you may know that 'there is none like unto the Lord our God.' " He promised that the frogs would leave the palace and the people's houses the next day and "remain in the river only."

FROGS IN THE PALACE

In making such a promise Moses took a great risk, but he believed God would do as He had said. And so it happened. In the morning the frogs were all dead. They "died out of the houses, out of the villages, and out of the fields." The people gathered them in heaps, "and the land stank." I am sure it did.

But when Pharaoh saw and smelled the dead frogs, and knew that the plague was over, he changed his mind and refused to keep his part of the bargain. The Bible says he "hardened his heart," which is a bad thing for anybody to do, and always leads to trouble.

And more trouble was on the way for Pharaoh.

"Stretch out thy rod, and smite the dust of the land," God said to Aaron, "that it may become lice throughout all the land of Egypt."

Aaron did so, and the dust "became lice in man, and in beast . . . throughout all the land of Egypt." That means there were lice in the palace also—on Pharaoh's servants, on his wife, on his children, and on himself.

His magicians, also tormented with lice, tried to imitate what Moses had done, but failed. "This is the finger of God," they said. But though these men were beginning to see that there was a power at work in Egypt far greater than any they had ever known, Pharaoh was as obstinate as ever. Again he hardened his heart.

Next time Moses and Aaron met him they brought more bad news. If he would not let the children of Israel go, they told him, then God would send swarms of flies, "and the houses of the Egyptians shall be full of swarms of flies."

This time, however, a difference would be made between Egypt and the land of Goshen, where the Hebrews lived. God would make a barrier between them. There would be no flies there.

"To morrow shall this sign be," said Aaron. And in the morning the flies were there, myriads of flies. They got in the people's eyes, in their clothes, in their food. There was no use killing them, for more and still more came, till everyone was frantic.

It was the same in the palace as in the home of the humblest Egyptian. Throne room, banqueting hall, and bedrooms were black with flies. At last Pharaoh couldn't endure any more of it. He sent for Moses and Aaron. "Go ye," he said, "sacrifice to your God in the land."

At last he was willing for the Hebrews to have time off for their sacrifice, but it must be in the land of Egypt.

Moses wouldn't agree. "No," he said, "we want to go to the wilderness."

"All right," said Pharaoh, driven to desperation. "Go if you must. Anything, so long as you get rid of these flies. Only, don't go very far away."

At this Moses promised to ask God to remove the flies, but as soon as he and Aaron were gone, Pharaoh hardened his heart yet again, "neither would he let the people go."

Moses and Aaron must have wondered what else would have to happen before this stubborn man would bow to the will of God. They did not have to wait long to find out.

STORY 8

Three Dark Days

IT IS surprising how many times some people have to be punished before they learn to do right.

You would think that after Pharaoh had seen all the water in Egypt turned to blood, after he had had frogs jumping all over his palace and swarms of lice and flies tormenting him to death, he would have come to see that the God of Moses and Aaron, who had sent these dreadful plagues, was not a God to be trifled with. But as soon as each plague ceased he hardened his heart again.

So he had to suffer some more.

Soon the cattle of Egypt began to die in droves, thousands of them. Then painful boils broke out on the people. Pharaoh got boils. So did his magicians, and all his servants. Next there came a frightful storm with thunder, lightning, and hail such as Egypt had never seen before. It broke down every tree and flattened the entire crop of flax and barley. Then came myriads of locusts, which ate every green thing that remained after the storm. The whole country must have looked like a desert.

This meant ruin and starvation to every Egyptian family. It meant ruin for the government too, for there would be no money for taxes. And while everybody was wondering what dreadful thing would happen next, a great darkness fell upon the land. The Bible says it was so dark that people couldn't see one another. For three days nobody left his house.

Everybody was frightened now, even Pharaoh himself. There was no sunshine by day, no moonlight at night. Even the stars were blacked out. The darkness was so dense it could be felt. Coming after all the other terrible happenings, it was just too much to bear.

At the end of the third dark day Pharaoh again sent for Moses and Aaron. Just how he found them we are not told. Perhaps two soldiers, holding torches aloft, made their way through the darkness to the land of Goshen, where, to their surprise, they found there was light in the homes of the children of Israel.

Through the pitch blackness Moses and Aaron were led to the palace. It must have been an eerie journey, for there was no traffic on the streets, no movement anywhere, only an awesome silence, broken by the barking of dogs and the cries of terrified children.

"Go!" said Pharaoh, angrily, as the two men came before him. "Go, serve the Lord!"

This time he was willing for all the Israelites to go, men, women, and children, but not their cattle. With all the cattle of Egypt killed, he naturally had his eye on the beauti-

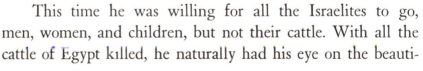

ful flocks and herds of the Hebrews, which had been spared.

But Moses would not agree. The Hebrews would take their cattle with them. They would need them for sacrifices, he said.

This made Pharaoh madder than ever.

"Get out!" he cried. "See my face no more; for in that day thou seest my face thou shalt die."

Moses was beginning to get angry now, and he said something full of meaning which Pharaoh did not understand— not then.

"Thou hast spoken well," he said, coldly. "I will see thy face again no more."

Then, with rising wrath, he told the king that one last terrible plague was about to fall upon him and his people.

"And Moses said, Thus saith the Lord, About midnight will I go out into the midst of Egypt: and all the firstborn in the land of Egypt shall die, from the firstborn of Pharaoh that sitteth upon his throne, even unto the firstborn of the maidservant that is behind the mill; and all the firstborn of beasts. And there shall be a great cry through all the land of Egypt. . . . And all these thy servants shall come down unto me, and bow down themselves unto me, saying, Get thee out, and all the people that follow thee: and after that I will go out. And he went out from Pharaoh in a great anger."

The darkness had passed by now, and as Moses strode through the streets with Aaron at his side, the people looked at them in awe. What men had ever been able to work such miracles before? What men had been able to see Pharaoh ten times in succession and come away alive? The Bible says, "The

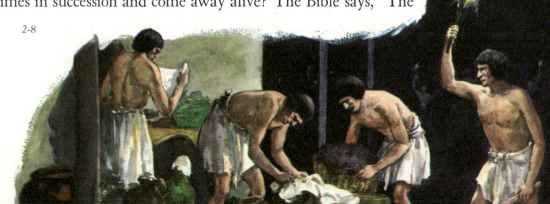

man Moses was very great in the land of Egypt, in the sight of Pharaoh's servants, and in the sight of the people."

Now things began to happen fast. Knowing that only a few hours remained before the great Exodus would begin, Moses gave orders that the Hebrews should visit the Egyptians and collect the wages they had not been paid for years. They were to ask for "jewels of silver, and jewels of gold." And the Egyptians paid up. They were too scared to do anything else.

Then word was sent from home to home through all the land of Goshen, to every Hebrew family: "This is the night of deliverance. Tonight God will smite all the first-born of Egypt. Pharaoh will then let us go. Pack your things. Prepare food for a long journey. Get ready to leave. Tomorrow we shall be on our way to freedom!"

Imagine the excitement everywhere. It all seemed too good to be true. Old men and women, who had toiled long years for the Egyptians, and had been beaten many times by the taskmasters, cried out with thankful hearts, "Thank God, thank God! It's over at last! God has kept His promise!"

Boys and girls looked up into their mother's face and asked, "Are we really going away, Mamma? Where to? To the land flowing with milk and honey you told us about?"

And when their mother said, "Yes, darlings, that's just where we are going," they cried out in glee, dancing and jumping around; "Oh, goody, goody, we're off to the land of Canaan!"

PART III

Stories of the Exodus

(Exodus 11:1-18:27)

STORY 1

Blood on the Doorposts

O N THAT last afternoon in Egypt every Hebrew father and mother had a secret worry. If it was true, as Moses said, that the angel of death was coming that night to smite all the first-born in the land, would he make no mistakes? Would he be sure to tell the difference between an Egyptian home and a Hebrew home? In the darkness, and with so many homes to visit, might he not enter one of them in error?

To make sure that the Hebrews would not suffer from this last awful plague, God told them to take the blood of a lamb and sprinkle it upon the doorposts of their homes. "And when I see the blood," He said, "I will pass over you."

All who believed that God was with Moses did as he said. They took a lamb or a baby he-goat, killed it, and smeared the blood on the doorposts of their homes. At sunset that evening the sprinkling of the blood was going on all through the land of Goshen, wherever a faithful Hebrew lived. Everywhere men

117

The night when Israel was to leave Egypt
very parent sprinkled the blood of a lamb
on the doorposts of his house to show he believed God would save his family from death.

and women asked each other, "Is the blood sprinkled on your home?" And if a home was seen to be without blood on its doorposts, neighbors would bang on the door, crying, "Don't forget the blood!"

It must have been quite a sight, with each family standing outside its home as the father, holding a basin of blood in one hand and a sprig of hyssop in the other, sprinkled first one doorpost and then the other. In every case the most interested onlooker was the eldest son, the first-born, whose life was at stake. You can be sure that he made certain the job was well done.

There may have been some who said, "Why do we have to sprinkle blood on our doorposts anyway? What good can this do us?" If so, they soon learned. It was dangerous not to put up God's sign of safety.

Thousands of lambs must have died that last evening that Israel spent in Egypt. Every one of them was a symbol of Jesus, "the Lamb of God, which taketh away the sin of the world." The blood sprinkled on the doorposts was likewise a symbol of the blood of Jesus which was "shed for many" and which "cleanseth us from all sin."

When we, like the Hebrews in Egypt, obey God's word, and do as He says; when we accept Jesus as our Saviour and, as it were, sprinkle His blood upon the doorposts of our hearts,

118

then He will forgive us our sins, and will pass over us in the day of judgment. This is what the apostle Paul meant when he said, "Christ our passover is sacrificed for us."

What happened to the lamb whose blood was sprinkled on the doorposts? It was roasted whole and eaten by the whole family. And it was eaten "in haste," with everybody fully dressed, ready to leave at a moment's notice.

Whether anybody slept that night I don't know. I doubt it. The Egyptians may have, for an hour or two, but not the Hebrews. Fathers and mothers were too busy packing and getting things ready for the long journey ahead of them. As for the children, they were far too excited. Everybody must have been eagerly waiting for the signal to go. Tired as they all were, this was no night for sleep.

Suddenly a dreadful sound rose on the midnight air. From all the land of Egypt came the screams of frightened women, mingled with the wailing of thousands of people mourning their dead. The Egyptians who had killed so many of the Hebrews' children were learning what it meant to lose their own.

"And it came to pass, that at midnight the Lord smote all the firstborn in the land of Egypt, from the firstborn of Pharaoh that sat on his throne unto the firstborn of the captive that was in the dungeon; and all the firstborn of cattle."

This was the last and most terrible of all the plagues, and it brought Pharaoh, finally, to his knees. The Bible says he "rose up in the night, he, and all his servants, and all the Egyptians; and there was a great cry in Egypt; for there was not a house where there was not one dead. And he called for Moses and Aaron by night, and said, Rise up, and get you forth from among my people, both ye and the children of Israel; and go, serve the Lord, as ye have said. Also take your flocks and your herds, . . . and be gone."

With death in every home in Egypt the people had no desire to keep the Hebrews any longer. They wanted them to go *now*. They were "urgent . . . , that they might send them out of the land in haste." They even heaped more silver and gold and clothing upon them in their anxiety for them to be gone. Anything the Hebrews asked for, they were given. So it was that "they spoiled the Egyptians."

That was one of the great nights of history, a night when a nation was born, a night when a million slaves became free, a night to be remembered through all time to come.

And it was on that night that God's promise to Abraham came true. Long ago He had told His faithful servant that after four hundred years his children would be delivered from Egyptian bondage. Now the time was up, and they were free again. Now they could go back to their homeland for which they had yearned so long.

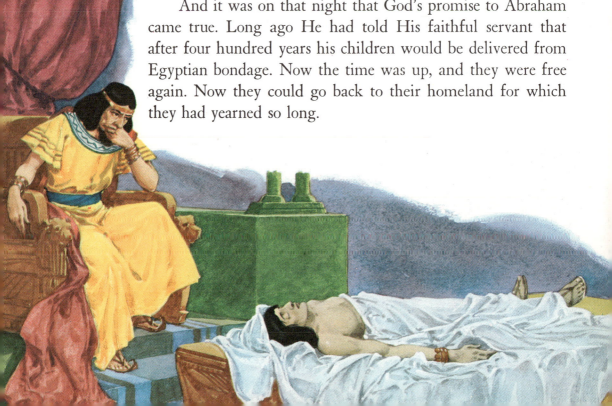

STORY 2

On to Freedom!

AS MORNING dawned it found all Egypt in deep mourning. The angel of death had entered every home. Thousands of bodies awaited burial, from that of the crown prince in the palace to the first-born of the humblest boatman on the Nile.

Meanwhile in the land of Goshen all was bustle and excitement. Most of the Hebrews had been awake all night. Now, as news spread that Pharaoh had at last agreed to let them go, their joy knew no bounds. Eagerly they clasped one anothers' hands and cried, "We're free, we're free!"

Some gloated over the piles of gold and silver ornaments they had collected from the Egyptians, wondering what they would do with so much wealth. Others knelt in prayer and thanked God for His protecting care through the night.

But there was no time to dally. Pharaoh might change his mind again, as he had nine times already. If they were going to leave Egypt, they must do so at once while the Egyptians were burying their dead.

121

ON TO FREEDOM!

Moses had already told the leaders of Israel where everybody was to meet, and soon all were making their way toward this place. Before sunrise thousands upon thousands of people were on the move, leaving their homes for good. Wagons, drawn by oxen, were loaded with tents, bedding, pots for cooking, jars of food, bundles of clothing, and other things they wanted to take along.

Some mothers had babies strapped to their backs, others had their "kneadingtroughs . . . bound up in their clothes on their shoulders." Had you been there, you might have seen a little boy carrying his pet puppy under one arm and trying to lead a young lamb with the other. You might have seen a little girl carrying a doll in one hand and holding her baby sister's hand in the other, for I am sure little girls had dolls back there just as they do now.

All kinds of people, old and young, grandpas and tiny tots, were in that moving crowd. Mixed up with them were animals of all sorts—cows, bulls, donkeys, sheep, goats, and dogs by the dozen. What the dogs did when they all got together I leave you to imagine.

As Moses stood watching the gathering of the people, with their flocks and herds, he may well have wondered how he would ever get so large a company safely to Canaan.

Now it was that his early training in the royal palace came in useful. Part of his education as a prince had been in the army, so he knew how to handle men and keep large numbers of people in order. Working through the leaders of Israel, he soon had the crowd forming into line and moving out along

123

— PAINTING BY HERBERT RUDEEN   ©   BY REVIEW AND HERALD

The great day of deliverance from Egyptian slavery had come at last, and there was great excitement. Everyone was eager to start on the journey through the wilderness to Canaan.

the route he planned to take them. Gradually a long procession took shape as the Hebrews started out for Canaan "five in a rank."

It must have taken hours just to get everything ready, for there were "six hundred thousand on foot that were men, beside children," "and flocks, and herds, even very much cattle."

And that wasn't all. Moses soon noticed that many people who were not Hebrews were joining the procession. The Bible calls them "a mixed multitude." Some of these no doubt were Egyptian servants who saw a chance to get away from their masters. Others may have been young people just looking for adventure. Whoever they were, they insisted on going along— and what a lot of trouble they caused later on! Many a time Moses must have wished he had stopped them at the beginning.

At last the whole great caravan was on its way. So long was it that those at the head could scarcely see those at the rear. Slowly, ever so slowly, it inched forward, gradually leaving behind Raamses and other cities that the Hebrews had helped to build. Smaller and smaller grew the pyramids until they were nothing more than specks on the horizon.

No doubt the young people and children wanted to travel much faster, but it was impossible. There were so many babies,

and no baby carriages in which to wheel them. There were so many sheep and goats and calves, and they couldn't be hurried. No doubt some men had a great deal of trouble trying to keep the flocks and herds moving at all. There would always be a cow or sheep wandering off by itself and having to be chased back into line.

Somewhere in the procession there was something that created quite a bit of excitement. It was a coffin. Among all his preparations for the Exodus, Moses had not forgotten Joseph's request that his bones be taken to Canaan.

At first nobody felt tired, not even the children. They were all so happy and excited to be leaving Egypt that they forgot how weary they really were. They had all been so busy getting ready for the journey and finding their right place in the procession that they had had no time to think that they were now homeless, without a place to sleep at night. They had been too busy also to worry about the future, or how they would get food and water in the desert through which they would have to pass. Even now all they wanted was to put as many miles as possible between themselves and Pharaoh—just in case he should change his mind and come after them. But as evening drew on and the children got tired and hungry, the fathers

and mothers began to wonder about some of these things.

How long would the journey take? When would they be able to settle down in their new homes in Canaan? Was there enough food for everybody? How about water? Would they meet any enemies along the way? Would there be wild animals in the desert?

Suddenly there was a shout that seemed to echo all down the long line of people.

"The cloud! Look at the cloud!"

They had been enveloped in clouds of dust all day, kicked up by the herds of cattle, but this was different. This was more like a pillar of cloud that went straight up, away ahead of the procession.

"See the cloud, Mamma!" cried the boys and girls. "See the cloud!"

"I see it!" said a thousand worried mothers. "But what is it? What does it mean?"

Then word passed down the line from Moses that God was in the cloud and would lead His people all the way they had to go.

As darkness came on, the cloud glowed with a light so beautiful that the people called it a pillar of fire. And it was wonderfully cheering, that first night away from home, to know that God was so near.

There was no need to worry any more, no need for any fears about the future. If the great God of Abraham, Isaac, and Jacob was leading them, all would be well. He would care for everything. He would bring them into Canaan safe and sound.

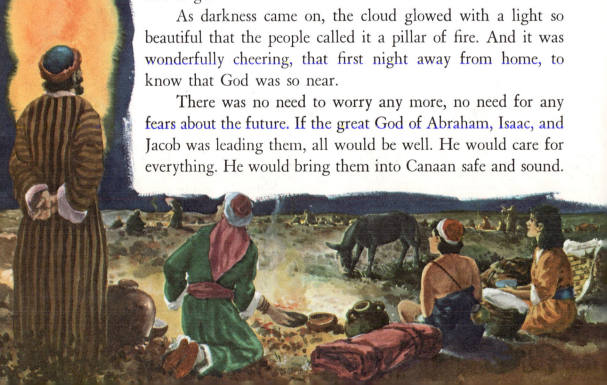

STORY 3

Walking Through the Sea

ARLY next morning, even before the sun was up, the children of Israel were astir. All wanted to get on their way as soon as they could.

As quickly as possible the animals were fed and the children were given their breakfast. Then, as the pillar of cloud moved slowly forward, those at the head followed it, and the caravan moved on.

Of course they all expected to go straight to Canaan, a journey that would have taken them only a few days at the most. But when they reached a little place called Etham, less than 150 miles from the border of Canaan, orders came from Moses that they were to turn south and "go through the way of the wilderness of the Red sea."

Everybody was surprised, and no doubt many said, "This isn't the way to Canaan."

But God had a purpose in leading His people this way. Had they gone direct to Canaan, they would have had to pass

127

through the land of the Philistines, who would have fought them. And God knew that if these poor people, just out of slavery, should see war too soon, they would lose heart and return to Egypt.

So on they went in the wrong direction, or so it seemed. You can imagine how the people watched the pillar of cloud all that day to see whether maybe it would turn back and go where they thought it should go. But it did not turn. Instead it moved slowly forward till it came to a place called Pi-hahiroth, on the shores of the Red Sea. Here Moses told the people to make camp for the night and rest.

There must have been a lot of talking as the people prepared their evening meal. I can almost hear someone saying, "Seems to me we're going to Ethiopia, not Canaan." And another, "Nice place to get caught, if the Egyptians should come after us, what with mountains on one side and the Red Sea on the other."

And many a little boy probably asked, "Daddy, are we going to sail over the sea in boats? Where are the boats?"

Suddenly a cry of alarm is heard. A man is pointing back along the way they have just come. Far in the distance a cloud of dust is rising. In the midst of it are moving figures. Men on horseback! Chariots! The Egyptians!

The very thing that the Hebrews most feared is happening. Pharaoh has changed his mind. Not only does he want revenge for the death of his son and for the death of so many of his subjects, but he wants his slaves back. He has forgotten the plagues, and he is determined to recover the

128

cattle, and gold and silver jewelry the Hebrews had taken away.

You see, when Pharaoh was told that the Hebrews had fled, taking all their cattle with them, he had found it hard to believe. But as the truth dawned upon him he had shouted, "Why have we done this, that we have let Israel go from serving us?"

"And he made ready his chariot, and took his people with him: and he took six hundred chosen chariots, and all the chariots of Egypt . . . and he pursued after the children of Israel . . . and overtook them encamping by the sea."

Now as the Hebrews see the chariots rushing toward them they are terrified. They know how cruel the Egyptians can be. They know what fate awaits them from their whips and swords and spears. They rush to Moses, and almost shriek at him in their fear, "Why did you bring us out here to die in this wilderness?"

It is a dark hour for Moses. He too has seen the Egyptians coming, and he knows full well what they will do to him if they catch him. But he is not afraid. He is sure that God has not brought His people this far to let them be killed by the Egyptians. He has not forgotten the great miracles God wrought but a week ago, and he is sure God will work another now if need be.

"Fear not!" he cries bravely to the people. "Fear ye not, stand still, and see the salvation of the Lord, which he will shew to you to day: for the Egyptians whom ye have seen to day, ye shall see them again no more for ever. The Lord shall fight for you, and ye shall hold your peace."

9

Even as Moses speaks something begins to happen. The pillar of cloud moves mysteriously toward the onrushing Egyptians, and becomes a barrier between them and the frightened Hebrews. As night falls, the cloud brings dense darkness to the Egyptians while shedding a warm, cheering glow upon the camp of Israel.

And now Moses, left alone, kneels in prayer to God, telling Him all that has happened. But this is not only a time for prayer, but for action.

"Wherefore criest thou unto me?" God says to him. "Speak unto the children of Israel, that they go forward."

Suddenly the wind begins to blow. And what a wind! It roars in from the east with great fury, throwing up huge clouds of sand in the desert

WALKING THROUGH THE SEA

and lashing the Red Sea into a foaming mass of white-capped waves.

Standing on the shore, his rod in his outstretched hand, Moses watches the tremendous sight. For this is no ordinary storm. God is working through the wind. He is cutting a path through the sea!

Down, down, goes the water until the sea bottom is uncovered! Now straight ahead, from shore to shore, is a wide strip of dry land.

"Forward!" cries Moses, knowing that God has made this way of escape for His people.

"Forward!" cry the leaders of Israel, passing on the word of command. "Forward! Everybody forward!"

I wonder who goes first? It takes courage, a lot of courage, with those towering walls of water on either side. What a pity we don't know! Perhaps it is a little boy, leading his dog. Perhaps it is a brave little girl, anxious to save her baby sister. I don't know. But *somebody* is first to step onto that strange, wind-swept avenue through the stormy sea.

Now another plucks up courage to go, and another, and another, while the rest line the shore in thousands awaiting their turn.

"Hurry! Hurry!" is the word on everybody's lips. For nobody knows when the wind will stop blowing. Nobody knows when the water will come crashing down again. Nobody knows when Pharaoh will discover what is going on and dash after them.

Now there are hundreds of people half walking, half running, along this path through the sea, with oxen, cows, donkeys, goats, sheep, and dogs moving forward with them as fast as they can, and getting in everybody's way.

It is a marvelous, never-to-be-forgotten sight—Moses standing tirelessly with rod outstretched, his long white beard blown this way and that by the raging wind; the dark green barricades of water, with foam and spray whirling up from their tossing summits; the anxious crowds rushing on to safety; a worried old man whacking a stubborn donkey; a frightened mother dragging her scared children; two careless boys throwing stones at the walls of water; and the whole amazing scene lighted up by the bright glow from the pillar of fire.

Could Israel ever forget this night?

STORY 4

Song of Victory

HOUR after hour the strange procession continues, with men, women, and children fleeing for dear life along the corridor God has made through the sea.

Drivers of wagons shout at their oxen, urging them to move faster. Dogs bark frantically at the herds of cattle and the flocks of sheep and goats as they try to make them run to the other shore. Mothers implore their little ones not to lag behind.

Ahead is the one hope of safety. Behind are the Egyptians, scarcely a mile away. Who can tell when they will discover everybody is escaping? And who can tell how long the water will remain piled up on either side, "congealed in the heart of the sea," as the Bible says it was?

On, on, on, they hurry, six hundred thousand men, besides women and children, dashing pell-mell for the other shore.

133

How long it took for so many to make the crossing we are not told. Finally, however, the last wagon has been helped up the opposite bank, the last father and mother has scrambled onto higher ground, the last dog has driven the last sheep out of the danger zone, and the last lost little boys and girls are safe with their parents again.

What a sigh of relief goes up from everybody as, looking back, they see the channel is clear! Everybody has got across! No one is left behind!

But look! What is that moving on the shore they have just left? Spears! Swords! Chariots! The Egyptians! See! They are rushing down the opposite bank! They are coming right through the channel between the walls of water!

"O God!" cry the people in their fear and anguish. "O God, help us! Save us from the Egyptians!"

All eyes are turned toward Moses, who is standing there erect, looking bravely, defiantly, at the oncoming hosts of Pharaoh. In his right hand is his rod stretched out once more over the wind-swept waters.

SONG OF VICTORY

Now something is happening in the channel. It is not so dry as it was. Pools of water are forming. And, oh, look! That first chariot has stopped! Its wheels have sunk in the mud. The driver is whipping his horses, trying to get them to pull it out, but it won't move.

Now another has bogged down, and another. Their wheels have come off!

The confusion grows worse and worse. Other chariots, trying to pass those in front, get all tangled up with the ones that have broken down. Angry shouts rise above the shrieking of the wind.

"Look out! Can't you see where you're going?"

"Go on, go on!" cry the officers. But they can't go on. The water is rising in the channel. The path through the sea is disappearing.

"Go back! Go back!" someone yells.

But it is too late. They cannot go back. There is no room to turn round. They are trapped.

"And it came to pass," the Bible says, "that in the morning watch the Lord looked unto the host of the Egyptians through the pillar of fire and of the cloud, and troubled the host of the Egyptians, and took off their chariot wheels, that they drave them heavily: so that the Egyptians said, Let us flee from the face of Israel; for the Lord fighteth for them against the Egyptians."

Now, as Moses holds his rod above the sea, the wind changes. At God's command it had cut this amazing path through the sea, and had kept it open while Israel passed through to safety; but now it causes the walls of water to come tumbling down, covering the chariots and drowning the soldiers.

"And the waters returned, and covered the chariots, and the horsemen, and all the host of Pharaoh that came into the sea after them; there remained not so much as one of them."

At sunrise the wind dies, and the sea becomes calm again. It is hard to believe that such a wonderful thing can have happened in this desert place. The distant mountains, the sandy beaches, the blue ribbon of water, are just the same as they were before. Nothing remains to remind Israel of God's great miracle but the bodies of the Egyptians washed up on the shore.

Yet these bodies tell a story that brings peace to all hearts. For the first time in their lives they do not have to worry about the Egyptians. They are gone forever. With Egypt ruined by the ten terrible plagues, and with Pharaoh's best troops drowned, the Israelites can forget the past and turn their faces bravely toward the future God is planning for them.

But listen! Someone is singing. Above the buzz of talking, the lowing of cattle, and the bleating of sheep comes a rich, deep voice in a song of praise to God. It is Moses! And what a song! Soon all the men are joining in, singing from their hearts:

"I will sing unto the Lord, for he hath triumphed gloriously: the horse and his rider hath he thrown into the sea. The Lord is my strength and song, and he is become my salvation: he is my God . . . my father's God, and I will exalt him. . . . Thou didst blow with thy wind, the sea covered them: they sank as lead in the mighty waters. Who is like unto thee, O

Lord, among the gods? who is like thee, glorious in holiness, fearful in praises, doing wonders?"

There is a pause. Then the women begin to sing, led by Miriam, Moses' sister, who watched over him, long ago, when he was a babe in that basket among the bulrushes. She has a "timbrel," or tambourine, in her hand which she plays as all the women take up the chorus, "Sing ye to the Lord, for he hath triumphed gloriously; the horse and his rider hath he thrown into the sea."

Everybody is so happy, happy beyond belief. Their old, ugly life in Egypt is past and gone forever. Their days of bondage are over. They are free! They are safe from their foes! And they would gladly stay right here by the Red Sea and keep on singing forever.

But Moses knows better. They have a long way to go. There are many mouths to feed. They must move on.

So when the song of praise is ended he gives orders for the caravan to be re-formed and made ready to start once more on its journey.

STORY 5

Food in the Desert

FOR three long, hot days the great caravan moved on through the wilderness.

People began to get tired and thirsty. The water they had brought along with them was almost gone. When children asked their parents for a drink they were told they couldn't have one. Those in charge of the cattle began to get worried about what would happen to the animals if water was not found soon.

Half a million men, besides women and children, can drink a lot of water on a warm day. So can thousands of cows, sheep, and goats. Water would have to be found, or they couldn't go on.

By the end of the third day many of the marchers were beginning to get worried. But presently somebody, scouting far ahead, began to wave excitedly. "Water!" he cried. "Water!"

The very word made everybody feel better. Spirits rose. They pressed forward eagerly.

139

Then came a great disappointment. When the first to reach the pool stooped down to drink of it, they found it bitter, and quite unfit to drink. Quickly the word sped back along the line. "The water's bad. We can't drink it." Marah, or "bitterness," they called the place.

Grumbling began. The people blamed Moses. Why had he brought them to such a spot? Didn't he know they would need water? Just as though Moses, who had lived in the wilderness for forty years, didn't know about the water problem!

"What shall we drink?" they cried.

As always, Moses took his troubles to God, and God had a way out. He pointed out a certain tree that, if cut down and thrown into the bitter water, would make it sweet. Moses did as he was told, and the water became fit to drink.

Next day the caravan moved on again, "and they came to Elim, where were twelve wells of water," and seventy palms to provide a little shade. "And they encamped there by the waters." Everybody was happy now. This was the first real rest they had had since leaving Egypt. After all the excitement,

the lack of sleep, and the long march they were just about worn out. So they were very glad for Elim, with its cool, fresh water and its palm trees.

Moses wisely decided to let them stay here for two or three weeks, and then ordered them to pack their tents and start on their way again. So "on the fifteenth day of the second month," just six weeks after leaving Egypt, they came into the Wilderness of Sin, about a hundred miles down the peninsula of Sinai.

It was a dry, barren, rocky country, with little pasture for the cattle and no place to grow food.

"What a place!" muttered some. "Why has he brought us here?"

"If we'd gone north instead of south, we would have been in Canaan by now," said others.

"What does he think we're going to grow here?" asked a farmer, comparing the dry, sandy soil with the rich loam of the Nile valley.

"And how does he think we're going to keep our cattle alive on this poor scrubland?" asked another.

Their complaints were catching and soon everybody was grumbling. Then as food supplies got lower and lower, "the whole congregation" turned on Moses and Aaron as they always did when in trouble.

Forgetting all the miracles God had wrought for them in Egypt, at the Red Sea, and at Marah, they cried out, "Would to God we had died by the hand of the Lord in the land of Egypt, when we sat by the flesh pots, and when we did eat

141

bread to the full; for ye have brought us forth into this wilderness, to kill this whole assembly with hunger."

It was a silly thing to say, but they had been slaves so long they didn't know any better. Even though they had seen God do many wonderful things for them, they still did not understand Him or trust Him. Their chief concern was how to get enough to eat. They thought they would be willing to be slaves again if only they could just smell those fleshpots once more.

Moses told God what the people were saying, and asked Him what to do. God promised that He would "rain bread from heaven."

That evening, just as the people were wondering what to eat, thousands of birds flew into the camp. They were quails, and they flew so low that it was easy to kill them. Everybody had a good supper, and some perhaps remembered to thank God for looking after them once more.

But what about breakfast? There were no stores where they might go and buy shredded wheat or corn flakes, and no milkman to leave milk outside each tent.

142

FOOD IN THE DESERT

What sort of food would God provide in the morning? many wondered. Would He send quails again? No. Instead, He sent something quite different. Early next day, as soon as the dew had gone, "behold, upon the face of the wilderness there lay a small round thing, as small as the hoar frost on the ground. And when the children of Israel saw it, they said one to another, It is manna. . . . And Moses said unto them, This is the bread which the Lord hath given you to eat."

How gingerly they picked up the first little piece with thumb and finger to taste it! But it was nice. It had a sweet taste, "like wafers made with honey," and they liked it. How good it must have seemed to all those poor, hungry people, especially the boys and girls!

Morning by morning, without fail, they found the manna there, right at their tent doors. All they had to do was to gather it up and eat it. For the next forty years this was their main source of food.

There was one strange thing about it, however. It appeared on the ground only six days a week. It was never there on the seventh day—not one little tiny piece.

Why? Because God wanted to teach these people to keep His Sabbath holy. Adam and Eve had kept the Sabbath in the beginning. So had Abraham, Isaac, and Jacob. When the children of Israel went into Egypt, at Joseph's invitation, they had kept it too; but when they had been made slaves they had not been able to keep it. During that time many came to think it didn't matter, that God didn't expect them to keep it any more. Some had even forgotten which day it was.

FOOD IN THE DESERT

So now, by the miracle of the manna, God sought to bring His people back into the right and true way. Every Friday, the sixth day, they were told to go out and gather a double portion of manna, enough to last over the Sabbath. Marvelously the manna gathered on Friday kept for two days; whereas when too much was gathered on other days it quickly spoiled. This, plus the fact that no manna appeared on the seventh day, let the people see which day God wanted them to keep as the Sabbath. There simply couldn't be any doubt about it. It was the seventh day and none other.

At first there were some who didn't believe God meant what He said. These went out "on the seventh day for to gather, and they found none." God was displeased with them, and said, "How long refuse ye to keep my commandments and my laws? See, for that the Lord hath given you the sabbath, therefore he giveth you on the sixth day the bread of two days; abide ye every man in his place, let no man go out of his place on the seventh day."

This lesson, taught once every week for forty years, forever fixed in the minds of the Israelites the right day on which to keep the Sabbath. By the manna God said to them 2,080 times (52 multiplied by 40), "This day, the seventh day, is My Sabbath." And He did so in order that they might never forget it, nor have any excuse for making a mistake about it.

They never did forget it. Even now—three thousand years later—they have not forgotten it. How could they? How could anybody?

10

ood was not easy to find in the wilderness, God sent manna from heaven every day. ut on the sixth day of the week He sent a ouble portion, to last them over the Sabbath.

STORY 6

Too Busy Doing Good

NO LONGER worried about food, Israel journeyed on down the peninsula of Sinai. Then the water problem came up again. By the time they reached Rephidim once more "there was no water for the people to drink." As usual, they blamed Moses.

"Give us water!" they cried. "Why did you bring us out of Egypt to kill us and our children and our cattle with thirst?" Some even asked, "Is the Lord with us or not?"

This time they were very angry, "and Moses cried unto the Lord, saying, What shall I do unto this people? they be almost ready to stone me."

Then God told Moses to take some of the leading men in the camp, "the elders of Israel," and go on ahead to a certain rock in Horeb. This rock he was to strike with his rod, and water would flow from it.

The group of leaders went ahead with Moses and saw him strike the rock. Water flowed from it in abundance, and again

146

the needs of the people and the cattle were supplied.

Hardly was this problem solved, however, when more trouble came—this time from the people of Amalek, who did not like to have the Israelites passing through their country. Maybe too they thought this was a good chance to steal some of their cattle. Anyhow, their soldiers swooped down out of the mountains one day, taking Israel by surprise. But they were quickly defeated, thanks to a young man named Joshua, who led the men of Israel into battle.

Moses watched the fight from a hilltop, with Aaron and Hur. After awhile these two men noticed that when Moses held up his hands, the soldiers of Israel advanced; but that when he dropped his hands, Amalek prevailed. So Aaron and Hur set Moses on a stone and held up his hands, "the one on the one side, the other on the other side," until victory was won.

By sunset the Amalekites were in flight, and Moses was able to rest his weary arms. Then he built an altar to the Lord, calling it Jehovah-nissi, meaning "the Lord my banner." The soldiers understood why. They had seen him holding up his hands in prayer to God for them all day—just as though he had been holding a banner to inspire them to do their best.

From Rephidim, Israel journeyed to the Wilderness of Sinai, and made camp near "the mount of God." Soon after this, word reached Moses that Jethro, his father-in-law, was coming to see him, bringing Zipporah, Moses' wife, and his two sons, Gershom and Eliezer.

Moses went out to meet Jethro, bowed respectfully to him, and kissed him. Then they all gathered together in Moses' tent to talk over all that had happened since Moses left Midian to go to Egypt.

I imagine those two boys were mighty glad to see their father again, don't you? And how surprised they must have been to see so many people! Having lived in the country all their lives, looking after their grandfather's sheep, they had never dreamed there were so many men, women, and children in all the world!

What a lot there was to talk about! "And Moses told his father in law all that the Lord had done unto Pharaoh and to the Egyptians for Israel's sake, and all the trials and difficulties that had come upon them by the way, and how the Lord delivered them.

"And Jethro rejoiced for all the goodness which the Lord had done to Israel." "Now I know," he said, "that the Lord is greater than all gods."

Then they had a big party for Jethro, with Moses, Aaron, and all the elders of Israel taking part.

Next morning Moses "sat to judge the people: and the people stood by Moses from the morning unto the evening."

There were so many matters on which the people needed advice and so many cases of misunderstanding between one man and another that Moses was kept talking and answering questions all day long.

Jethro stood by, watching and listening. When at last he was able to speak to Moses alone, he gave him some good advice.

"You can't stand this," he said. "You'll wear yourself out."

"But," said Moses, "the people keep coming to me, and I have to judge between them and make them know the statutes of God and His laws."

"But it's too much for you," said Jethro. "You cannot do all this by yourself."

Then he told Moses to divide the work and lay some of the burden upon others. "Provide out of all the people able men," he said, "such as fear God, men of truth, hating covetousness; and place such over them, to be rulers of thousands, and rulers of hundreds, rulers of fifties, and rulers of tens: and let *them* judge the people at all seasons: and it shall be, that every great matter they shall bring unto thee, but every small matter they shall judge: so shall it be easier for thyself, and they shall bear the burden with thee."

It was good advice. Moses, with the best intentions in the world, was trying to do too much. He was actually too busy doing good. He liked being thought of as the father of his people, meeting all their needs and answering all their questions. But nobody could do all this and keep well. As Jethro said, he was just wearing himself out and would die long before his work was done.

Fortunately Moses was humble enough to take advice—which is more than can be said of some boys and girls I know. He did what Jethro said, and "chose able men out of all Israel, and made them heads over the people, rulers of thousands, rulers of hundreds, rulers of fifties, and rulers of tens. And they judged the people at all seasons: the hard causes they brought unto Moses, but every small matter they judged themselves."

It was a good thing that Moses did as he was told, for big events were about to happen. In just a little while he would have to spend forty days and forty nights with God on Mount Sinai. Had he not given up all his detail work as judge and counselor of the people, he would never have been able to do the far greater things God wanted him to do. He would have been too busy to seize life's greatest opportunities, too busy to receive the tables of the law from its holy Author, too busy to meet God face to face.

It pays to take advice from a good man.

PART IV

Stories of Moses and the Tabernacle

(Exodus 19:1 to Leviticus 8:36)

STORY 1

Ten Golden Rules

T HREE months after the children of Israel had been
delivered from Egyptian bondage they were encamped,
not in Canaan, but in a very hot desert in the shadow
of Mount Sinai.

Instead of going north, the pillar of cloud had moved
south; and here they were, hundreds of miles from where
they had expected to be at this time.

Why had God done this?

First, because He knew that His people, just freed from
centuries of slavery, were not ready to meet the warlike Philistines who lived in the southern part of Palestine.

Second, because He had some lessons He wanted to teach
them, and for this He needed time and a private place, shut
off from the rest of the world.

Third, and most important of all, He was planning a great
future for these people, and He wanted to have them all to
Himself for a while until He was sure they understood what

153

The first four commandments of the Decalogue
teach us our duty to God, and the last six our
duty to men. This wonderful law given to
Israel through Moses has never been changed.

sort of people He wanted them to be and what kind of work He wanted them to do.

For God had not brought the children of Israel out of Egypt by such a wonderful deliverance just so they could be like other nations. They were to be totally different. Someday, through them, would come the "seed of the woman" (Jesus) to crush the serpent's head. Therefore He wanted them to be His chief helpers in making known His plan of salvation to all people. They, above all, were to tell the story of His love for this world—how He created it in the beginning, and how He plans to restore it to its Edenic beauty someday in the future.

If they were to be His witnesses, speaking to others of a holy God, they too must be holy. They must know right from wrong and be glad and willing to choose the right at all times. They must know why sin is hateful—and hate it.

But how could they be a holy people when they knew so little of what God expected of them? True, some knowledge of His laws and standards had come down to them through Abraham, Isaac, Jacob, Joseph, and their own parents; but during the long, sad years of bondage in Egypt, when they had had to live and work among idolaters, many of God's teachings had been forgotten.

Because God knew all this, He spoke again from Sinai, making known His will so clearly that there could be no

mistake or misunderstanding about it through all time to come. Before He did so, however, He told Moses to tell the people to sanctify themselves and "wash their clothes." This was to be a very solemn occasion, which they would not forget as long as they lived.

"Be ready against the third day," said Moses: "for the third day the Lord will come down in the sight of all the people upon mount Sinai."

Great excitement filled the camp. The mighty God who had saved them from the Egyptians, who had cut a path through the sea, and who had sent them bread from heaven and water from the rock, the wonderful God of whom they had talked and dreamed from childhood, was coming near to them, so near they would be able to hear His voice.

The days of preparation quickly passed. Then on the morning of the third day Mount Sinai became like a volcano, its summit enveloped in a fiery cloud. "There were thunders and lightnings, and a thick cloud upon the mount. . . . And mount Sinai was altogether on a smoke, because the Lord descended upon it in fire: and the smoke thereof ascended as the smoke of a furnace, and the whole mount quaked greatly."

It was an awesome sight, and the children of Israel trembled with fear. Even the boys and girls stood silent and still as they gazed at the mighty spectacle in wide-eyed wonder.

Suddenly, from far up on the mount, out of the midst of the fire and the smoke, came a wondrous sound, deep, rich, melodious. It was the voice of God.

155

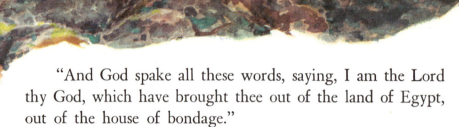

"And God spake all these words, saying, I am the Lord thy God, which have brought thee out of the land of Egypt, out of the house of bondage."

Then He declared His holy will in the Ten Commandments:

1. "Thou shalt have no other gods before me."

2. "Thou shalt not make unto thee any graven image, or any likeness of any thing that is in heaven above, or that is in the earth beneath, or that is in the water under the earth: thou shalt not bow down thyself to them, nor serve them: for I the Lord thy God am a jealous God, visiting the iniquity of the fathers upon the children unto the third and fourth generation of them that hate me; and shewing mercy unto thousands of them that love me, and keep my commandments."

3. "Thou shalt not take the name of the Lord thy God in vain; for the Lord will not hold him guiltless that taketh his name in vain."

4. "Remember the sabbath day, to keep it holy. Six days shalt thou labour, and do all thy work: but the seventh day is the sabbath of the Lord thy God: in it thou shalt not do

any work, thou, nor thy son, nor thy daughter, thy man-servant, nor thy maidservant, nor thy cattle, nor thy stranger that is within thy gates: for in six days the Lord made heaven and earth, the sea, and all that in them is, and rested the seventh day: wherefore the Lord blessed the sabbath day, and hallowed it."

5. "Honour thy father and thy mother: that thy days may be long upon the land which the Lord thy God giveth thee."

6. "Thou shalt not kill."

7. "Thou shalt not commit adultery."

8. "Thou shalt not steal."

9. "Thou shalt not bear false witness against thy neighbour."

10. "Thou shalt not covet thy neighbour's house, thou shalt not covet thy neighbour's wife, nor his manservant, nor his maidservant, nor his ox, nor his ass, nor any thing that is thy neighbour's."

As the people listened they were greatly moved. That lovely voice, speaking with such majesty and power, yet with a tenderness they had never heard before, touched every heart. It made them want to be good. If this was the will of God, then they wanted to do it. So "they answered together, and said, All that the Lord hath spoken will we do." Three times they said it, and I believe they meant it.

But God knew how soon they would forget, and that some would begin to question what it was He had said. So, because these commandments were His will, not only for the

Israelites, but for all mankind, and in order that men should know that they are unchangeable, He wrote them on two slabs of stone. The Bible says that "he gave unto Moses, when he had made an end of communing with him upon mount Sinai, two tables of testimony, tables of stone, written with the finger of God."

God wrote them himself, with His own finger! How very important they must be!

Jesus thought so too. When, long years after that wonderful scene at Sinai, our loving Saviour came to teach us how to live, and once again revealed the mind and will of God, He said, "Till heaven and earth pass, one jot or one tittle shall in no wise pass from the law, till all be fulfilled."

And He added these solemn words: "Whosoever therefore shall break one of these least commandments, and shall teach men so, he shall be called the least in the kingdom of heaven: but whosoever shall do and teach them, the same shall be called great in the kingdom of heaven."

Today these ten golden rules are still God's will for us. All who love Him truly will try their best to keep them with His help. From their hearts they will say with gladness, like the Israelites of old, "All that the Lord hath said will we do, and be obedient."

STORY 2

Israel's "Traffic" Laws

AFTER God had spoken from Sinai, telling the children of Israel His ten golden rules of life, Moses gave them many other laws so that they could live together peacefully in the camp.

Just as we have traffic laws today telling us how fast we may drive on the highway, what we must do when a school bus stops, how far we must keep behind a fire engine, and what must be done when one car bumps into another, so Israel was given all sorts of regulations about how they were to act toward one another.

Unlike God's Ten Commandments which, of course, never change and apply to everybody in all the world, Israel's "traffic" laws are today mostly out of date. Yet they were very important at the time, for these people had been living as slaves for many, many years, and didn't know how to behave as free men and women. Some of them even believed in slavery. They didn't know any better.

159

God had to educate them, and so, through Moses, He taught them first one lesson, then another. He couldn't change their thinking all at once, so He did it little by little.

For instance, knowing how some of them thought about slavery, He gave orders, through Moses, that if anyone bought a slave, then, after six years of service, the slave should "go out free for nothing." That was a start, at least, toward full freedom.

There were other interesting laws like this.

If two men got into a fight and one struck the other with his fist or a stone, and hurt him so badly he had to go to bed, then the one who struck the blow had to cause the other man to be "thoroughly healed" and "pay for the loss of his time." That was very fair, and no doubt saved quite a number of fights.

If a man dug a pit and forgot to put a cover on it, and another man's ox or ass fell into it and was killed, then the man who dug the pit had to pay the other man the value of the dead animal. This also was very fair, don't you think?

If a man put his cattle or sheep to feed in a neighbor's field, then he had to give that neighbor "of the best of his own field."

If one man's ox hurt another man's ox so badly that it died, then the live ox had to be sold and the money divided. The dead ox was also divided—and so both parties were satisfied.

Another thing Moses told them was that they were never to take a bribe, for, he said, a bribe makes people tell untruths. How true!

"Thou shalt not oppress a stranger" was another very fine law, and the reason given was, "For ye know the heart of a stranger, seeing ye were strangers in the land of Egypt."

Day after day Moses tried to teach the people all these lessons in how to behave. No doubt they had many questions. Some asked him, "What shall we do in this case, and what shall we do in that?" Through the leaders of thousands, and hundreds, and fifties, and tens, he tried to answer them and show them the right way.

I suppose everybody didn't like what he told them. Some preferred to do as they had done before. Maybe some said, "Why should we bother about what he says?" But the leaders tried their best to enforce the new "traffic" laws, and gradually the people came to understand that obedience was the better way. But it must have been a struggle.

Then one day Moses called the leaders together and told them that God had asked him to come up into the mount again, bringing Joshua with him. "Tarry ye here for us," he said, "until we come again unto you: and, behold, Aaron and Hur are with you: if any man have any matters to do, let him come unto them."

11

So Aaron and Hur were left in charge of the camp, while Moses and Joshua waved the leaders farewell and climbed slowly up toward the summit of Sinai.

"And the glory of the Lord abode upon mount Sinai. . . . And the sight of the glory of the Lord was like devouring fire on the top of the mount in the eyes of the children of Israel. And Moses went up into the midst of the cloud."

As Moses and Joshua disappeared, Aaron and the others who were with him turned back toward the camp, wondering how long their leader would be away and what might happen to him up there with God.

He had said he would return. But would he? How could any human being live in the midst of that devouring fire? What if he never came back? What would happen to all the people? How could they find their way to Canaan without him?

It was not long before others in the camp began to ask the same questions. Then as day succeeded day and there was no sign of Moses, everybody became more and more worried about him. One week, two weeks, three weeks went by, and still there was no word out of the cloud.

"He must be dead," they said. "We had better return to Egypt."

STORY 3

Moses on the Mount

MOSES stayed on the top of Mount Sinai almost six weeks, "forty days and forty nights."

What was he doing all that time? Something very important. He was listening to God, and a very wonderful story he heard.

God told him that He planned to dwell with Israel and wanted them to build a home for Him. "Let them make me a sanctuary;" He said, "that I may dwell among them."

It wasn't to be a great palace or a massive temple, but just a plain-looking tent, or "tabernacle." Yet every part of it was to be made with perfection. And every part was to mean something special and teach some beautiful lesson.

That's why Moses stayed so long. God was so anxious that His tabernacle should be made just right that He told him every little detail of what he was to do. And Moses must have written it all down; otherwise, he would never have remembered so much.

The building was to be something like God's dwelling place in heaven. Not that God expected Moses to make anything so magnificent and glorious as that. He couldn't have done so, however hard he had tried. But he was to follow the same general plan. The earthly sanctuary was to be a miniature of the heavenly sanctuary, and the services to be held in it were to correspond—in a small, human, earthly way—to those in God's dwelling place on high. "See," said God, "that thou make all things according to the pattern."

Of course, God didn't need a dwelling place for Himself. But the people needed it for their good. Here God would teach them more lessons they needed to learn. Here He would try to help them understand how much He loved them and how great a sacrifice He was prepared to make for their salvation. Here He would help them to see how much He hates sin, and how they could get rid of it, and become the pure, godly, righteous people He wanted them to be.

The sanctuary, or tabernacle, was to be portable, so that it could be carried from place to place as the children of Israel moved on their way to Canaan. The sides were to be of wood, lined with pure gold. The roof was to be of four different coverings, the inner one being of fine linen dyed blue, purple, and scarlet; the second of goats' hair; the third of rams' skins dyed red; and the outside one of badgers' skins.

Fifty-five feet long, by eighteen feet wide, by eighteen feet high, the tabernacle was to be divided into two apartments, which God called the holy place and the most holy place. These were to be separated by another curtain of blue,

164

purple, and scarlet, with figures of angels woven into it.

God asked for very little furniture. In the holy place there was to be nothing but a table for bread, an altar on which incense was to be burned, and a seven-branched candlestick for light.

The bread—or shewbread, as it was called—would remind the people that God would supply all their needs, and so point forward to Jesus, the Bread of Life. The sweet-smelling incense would tell them that their prayers, mingled with the fragrance of Jesus' love, would always be heard by God. And the light of the candlestick, which was never to be allowed to go out, would remind them that the light of truth shines on forever, even as Jesus, the Light of the world, lives forever.

Inside the most holy place Moses was to put a beautiful box, or ark, made of shittim wood overlaid with gold, to hold the tables of stone bearing the Ten Commandments. Above this he was to put a golden slab to be called the mercy seat, with two golden angels looking down reverently upon it. Here God Himself would appear in a holy light.

When you stop to think of it, that was a most beautiful thing that God did—to place a mercy seat between Himself and His law. He wanted His people to know that, though they might break His law, He would always be ready to for-

give them, if only they would repent and ask His pardon.

Then God told Moses of the services that were to be carried on in the tabernacle, and why animals were to be offered as sacrifices. This was not because God took pleasure in suffering, but because He wanted the children of Israel to learn how terrible is sin in His sight, and that death is its penalty. So the sinner must kill an innocent lamb to show he agreed that he deserved to die but offered the lamb in his stead. In this lamb he would see Jesus, someday to die on Calvary, "the Lamb of God, which taketh away the sin of the world."

Thus day after day, for forty days and forty nights, God told Moses what He wanted him to do, even naming those whom He wanted to be His priests, and describing the beautiful garments they were to wear. Then, on the last day, He gave Moses a very wonderful present. "And he gave unto Moses, when he had made an end of communing with him upon mount Sinai, two tables of testimony, tables of stone, written with the finger of God."

What a treasure! Imagine what those "tables of stone" would be worth today! Billions of dollars couldn't buy them. "And the tables were the work of God, and the writing was the writing of God, graven upon the tables."

Taking them in his arms, Moses began to descend the mountain, his whole being deeply moved by all that had happened. Think of spending six weeks alone with God! And then to receive from His hands the priceless tables of His law! He must have felt he was walking on air as he climbed down the rocky path to where Joshua had been waiting.

167

uring the journey of the children of Israel
rough the wilderness, God called Moses to
e top of Mount Sinai and gave him the Ten
ommandments, written on tables of stone.

Then came a terrible shock. Said Joshua, "There is a noise of war in the camp."

Moses stopped and listened. "It is not the voice of them that shout for mastery," he said, "neither is it the voice of them that cry for being overcome: but the noise of them that sing do I hear."

They hurried on, wondering what could be going on.

Suddenly, as they turned a corner of the trail, they saw what it was. In the midst of the camp was a golden calf, and the children of Israel were dancing around it!

The sight was too much for Moses. "No!" I can hear him saying. "Not this! Not idolatry! Not in so short a time!"

But it was even so.

In less than six weeks the people had turned away from God, after pledging to serve Him faithfully forever.

Terribly disappointed and fiercely angry, Moses cast the precious tables of stone from his hands. Smashed into a thousand pieces, they went clattering down the mountainside.

STORY 4

Trouble in the Camp

AS MOSES strode into the camp, his face aglow from the wonderful time he had spent with God on the mountain, his eyes blazing with anger at sight of the golden calf, the people fell back from him in awe. Those who had been dancing around the idol ran to find clothes to cover themselves. They were all afraid. They knew they had done wrong.

Sheepishly Aaron came forward.

"What does this mean?" demanded Moses. "I left you in charge; what did they do to you that you brought so great a sin upon them?"

Aaron hardly knew what to say.

"Don't be too angry with me," he said. "You know these people are set on mischief. They came to me and said, Make us gods, which shall go before us; for as for this Moses, the man that brought us up out of the land of Egypt, we don't know what has become of him."

169

It was a lame excuse and shows how much weaker Aaron was than Moses. It shows too how little the people really understood God or His commandments, which, six weeks before, they had promised so faithfully to obey.

"What about the idol?" Moses asked. "How did that come to be there?"

Aaron tried to explain. The people had brought gold to him, he said, and then added, "I cast it into the fire, and there came out this calf."

But an idol doesn't just come out of a fire. Aaron knew better than that. God does not work a miracle to make an idol. Somebody has to make a mold, and pour in the molten metal. This was no accident, but deliberate, shameful sin.

"Light a fire!" demanded Moses.

They did, and when it was hot he threw the golden calf into it. He let all the people see their poor little make-believe god melting away. When the metal was cool he called for hammers and set men to work beating it out into paper-thin sheets. The whole camp heard the noise, and everybody watched

as the gold spread out ever farther and farther under the endless rain of blows.

Bang! Clang! Bang! Clang! Bang! Clang!

Hour after hour the beating went on. Israel would not soon forget what God thought about idols.

When the gold had been beaten as thin as possible, Moses called for grinders to be brought—the big stones that the people used to grind their corn.

The people watched in amazement. "What's he going to do now?" they asked. "Grind gold?"

Just that. He broke up the paper-thin sheets into pieces and gave them to the men with the grindstones.

"Now grind!" he commanded. "Grind!"

Round and round and round went the great stones as the gold was crushed into ever smaller and smaller fragments.

"How long shall we grind?" asked some.

"Grind on!" Moses insisted. And grind they did until the gold of the golden calf had become nothing but the finest dust.

Probably the people expected that, having destroyed the golden calf so completely, Moses would just throw the dust away. But no! He had the grinders gather it up and put it in a bowl. Then he strode toward the place where the stream of water poured from the rock at the base of Mount Sinai. The people followed, frightened and wondering.

Then they saw Moses cast some of the gold dust into the water. Then more and more. The water turned red, as it does when gold is mixed with it. Suddenly a cry of alarm arose.

171

"Blood!" they cried. "The water has turned to blood!"

"Drink it!" commanded Moses. "Everybody drink it!"

They came and, stooping, drank of the blood-red stream.

The time had come for a showdown. Things could not go on like this. The rebels might take over the camp, and spoil all that God was trying to do for Israel. They must be punished severely, and at once.

So Moses stood at the gate of the camp and cried, "Who is on the Lord's side?"

It was an exciting moment. Would anybody answer? Was anybody on His side?

There was a stirring in the camp. People came running— old men, young men.

"We are!" they cried. "We are on the Lord's side!"

The first to come were the sons of Levi. Moses told them to take their swords and go through the camp from gate to gate, slaying the rebels, not sparing even one.

It was a sad, sad hour. Three thousand people were killed, all of whom had passed through the Red Sea and expected to go on to Canaan. Now they were dead. What a price they paid for worshiping that golden calf!

STORY 5

Face to Face With God

THAT night there was much sadness and fear in the camp. The people had just buried their dead, and they were wondering what other punishment might come upon them because of their terrible sin in worshiping the golden calf.

Not since their last night in Egypt had they seen so much death, and then it was the Egyptians who had suffered. Now three thousand of their own had been killed in one day— and who could tell how many more might have to die?

Moses was worried too, for He knew God was greatly displeased. In the morning he called the people together and said to them, "Ye have sinned a great sin: and now I will go up unto the Lord; peradventure I shall make an atonement for your sin."

With a heavy heart he climbed Mount Sinai again. As he entered the cloud and found himself in the presence of God, he cried out, "Oh, this people have sinned a great sin,

and have made them gods of gold. Yet now, if thou wilt forgive their sin—; and if not, blot me, I pray thee, out of thy
book which thou hast written."

One can almost hear the sob in his voice. That broken
sentence, "if thou wilt forgive their sin—" tells how deep was
the hurt in his heart. And when he said, "If not, blot me,
I pray thee, out of thy book," he was asking God to let him
die instead of his people, offering himself as a sacrifice that
they might live. Of course God would never have let him
do that, but He must have been pleased with the devotion
of His faithful servant.

"Whosoever hath sinned against me," said God, "him
will I blot out of my book."

For a moment Moses must have wondered whether God
was going to kill all the people for what they had done. But
in His great mercy He said, "Go, lead the people unto the
place of which I have spoken unto thee: behold, mine Angel
shall go before thee."

So Israel would have another chance.

174

"And the Lord spake unto Moses face to face, as a man speaketh unto his friend."

This does not mean that Moses actually saw the face of God. As God said to him once, "Thou canst not see my face: for there shall no man see me, and live." But it does mean that God and Moses were so very close to each other that they talked back and forth like very dear friends.

They were indeed so close and understood each other so well that Moses longed to see Him.

"I beseech thee," he once prayed, "shew me thy glory."

And God replied, "I will make all my goodness pass before thee, and I will proclaim the name of the Lord before thee."

Moses wanted to know where and how this would happen, and God replied, "While my glory passeth by, I will put thee in a clift of the rock, and will cover thee with my hand."

One day God said to him, "Be ready in the morning, and come up . . . unto mount Sinai, and present thyself there to me in the top of the mount." He was told to bring with him two tables of stone just like those he had broken, and God would write His law on them again.

So early the next morning Moses climbed the mountain once more, carrying the two tables of stone. "And the Lord descended in the cloud, and stood with him there, and proclaimed the name of the Lord."

As he stood in the cleft of the rock he felt God nearer than ever, and as the Lord passed by he heard a glorious voice saying: "The Lord, The Lord God, merciful and gracious, longsuffering, and abundant in goodness and truth, keeping mercy for thousands, forgiving iniquity and trans-gression and sin, and that will by no means clear the guilty; visiting the iniquity of the fathers upon the children, and upon the children's children, unto the third and to the fourth generation."

Quite overcome, Moses did not try to see God, as he had planned, or even to get a glimpse of Him. Instead, rev-erently, he "made haste, and bowed his head toward the earth, and worshipped."

Like Moses, many boys and girls want to see the face of God. And it is good that we should want to see Him. But we cannot, not yet. Someday, if we are very good, we shall see His face, but not now, nor do we need to. It is enough to know that He is merciful, kind, and forgiving, and "abun-dant in goodness and truth."

As the apostle John once said, "God is love"—and be-cause He is love we can trust Him fully even though we cannot actually see Him with our eyes.

Just like Moses, we can feel Him very close to us, "face to face" as it were, His face against ours, as we talk together like dearest friends.

STORY 6

Called by Name

WHEN Moses came down from Mount Sinai this time, after spending another forty days and forty nights with God, his face shone with a strange and wonderful light. It was so bright that even his own brother Aaron was afraid to come near him. So were the rest of the people. Before he could talk with them, he had to cover his face with a veil. Maybe if we lived close to God as long as Moses did, our faces would shine too!

Things were different in the camp now. There was no golden calf this time. The people had learned their lesson. They were now ready to build the sanctuary that God had told Moses about some weeks before. But first they were given a test to see how much they really cared for Him.

Moses asked them to bring God an offering of gold, silver, brass, jewels, spices, oil, fine linen, and skins of various kinds.

He knew the people had all these things, and that they had taken most of them from the Egyptians during their last night in bondage. He could have reminded them that they wouldn't have had any of this wealth if God had not delivered them, and that it all really belonged to Him. But he didn't. Instead, he told them that God wanted only gifts from people who were willing to give. If anybody didn't feel like giving, that was all right with Him; they could keep their things.

"Whosoever is of a willing heart, let him bring it, an offering of the Lord," he said. Nobody else.

As "the congregation of the children of Israel departed from the presence of Moses," the faithful old leader must have wondered what they would do. Up to now God had given them everything they had. This was the first time they had ever been asked to give anything to Him. How would they take it?

No doubt he watched their faces. Some looked pleased that they could do something to say Thank you to God for all His goodness to them. Others looked glum, telling themselves that if they parted with their valuables now, they would never get any more, not in this desert.

All went to their tents. Soon, in little groups, they be-

gan to come back to where Moses stood waiting for them.

I don't know who got back to him first, but it could have been a little boy, bringing some precious trinket that an Egyptian had given him. Or it might have been a little girl with a silver bracelet she treasured very much. Boys and girls run so much faster than older people that they *could* have been first, couldn't they? And how children do love to give what they can to God!

And if some of the children did get there before the others, I am sure Moses gave them a wonderful smile of thankfulness. There may have been tears in his eyes too at the thought that the children loved God best.

Then came the rest. From all parts of the camp they streamed toward Moses, bringing whatever they felt they could spare.

"And they came, every one whose heart stirred him up, and every one whom his spirit made willing, and they brought the Lord's offering. . . . And they came, both men and women, as many as were willing hearted, and brought bracelets, and earrings, and rings, and tablets, all jewels of gold. . . . And every man, with whom was found blue, and purple, and scarlet, and fine linen, and goats' hair, and red skins of rams, and badgers' skins, brought them. Every one that did offer an offering of silver and brass brought the Lord's offering: and every man, with whom was found shittim wood . . . , brought it." And so on and so on. It seemed as though somehow, somewhere, the people found everything that was needed. That's what a willing spirit does.

179

It must have been a wonderful sight, everybody bringing what he could, everybody helping the best way he knew how. And all the people looked so happy about it. Giving to God made them feel good all over.

When all the gifts were in, and piled up around Moses, he told them more of his plans for the building of the sanctuary.

First, he announced the name of the man who would be in charge of the work.

"The Lord hath called by name Bezaleel the son of Uri, the son of Hur, of the tribe of Judah."

If there was one surprised man in the camp at that moment, it was surely Bezaleel. And he would have been even more surprised had he known that God had actually mentioned him by name to Moses on the top of Mount Sinai.

He came forward blushing. A young craftsman, he wasn't used to anything like this. Certainly he had never expected any such honor. What could God need of him?

Then he learned something. He discovered how much God knew about him.

Pointing to him, Moses said, "He [the Lord] . . . hath filled him with the spirit of God, in wisdom, in understanding, and in knowledge, and in all manner of workmanship; and to devise curious works, to work in gold, and in silver, and in brass, and in the cutting of stones, to set them, and in carving of wood, to make any manner of cunning work. And he hath put in his heart that he may teach."

What a youth! He couldn't have been very old, for he was the grandson of Hur, who had held up Moses' hands in the battle with the Amalekites only a few weeks before. Yet he was filled with the Spirit of God; he was wise; he was a skilled workman in both metal and wood; he was a jeweler and a wood carver; and, most important of all, he could teach others how to do all these things.

Few people knew that there was anybody like this in the camp. But God knew that He needed a good man for a big job, and He said, "I want Bezaleel." He called him by name, so there would be no mistake.

It just shows how much God knows about all of us. He knows what we can do, what kind of training we have had, what kind of spirit is in our hearts. And He knows our names.

What do you suppose He knows about you? Will He ever call you to do a big job for Him?

STORY 7

Building the Tabernacle

FOR the next three months the camp of Israel was like a beehive. Everybody was busy—and happy. Having lots to do made them forget their troubles.

Young Bezaleel was right on the job, leading out in all the plans for building the tabernacle. Helping him was a group of other young people almost as skilled as he, and all *volunteers*. Of everyone it is said that his heart "stirred him up to come unto the work to do it." No wonder these volunteers did such a beautiful job! When people's hearts get "stirred up"—when they truly love their work—there's no limit to what they can do.

These men, we are told, "received of Moses all the offering, which the children of Israel had brought for . . . the sanctuary." In other words, Moses turned over to them the piles and piles of gifts that the people had brought to him, and the very first thing they had to do was to sort everything out.

182

BUILDING THE TABERNACLE

Things made of gold went into one bin, those made of silver into another, and pieces of brass went into a third. The many kinds of precious stones made a sorting job of its own. Then the goats' skins, the rams' skins, and the badgers' skins, all had to be put in separate places, as also the linen, the spices, the dyes, and all the rest. When a million people begin giving, there's no knowing what will turn up.

The sorting wasn't made any easier by the fact that, having begun to give, the people didn't want to stop. "Every morning" they lined up with more and more gifts, until the sorters didn't know what to do with all the stuff.

"Tell them to stop!" they begged Moses. "We have far too much already!"

Moses came to see for himself, and found the report was only too true. So he sent messengers through the camp telling the people not to bring anything more.

I wouldn't be surprised if some were disappointed. I can imagine some little boy saying, "Mamma, I was just going to give that silver coin I've been saving all this time, and now they don't want it!" and his mamma saying, "It's too late now, son. You should have given it before."

Or a little girl may have said, "Mamma, I had just about made up my mind to give my pretty necklace—you know, the one with the emeralds in it."

Then her mamma replied, "You should have made up your mind earlier. Now it's too late."

It *was* too late, too late for anybody else to have a part in giving to God's sanctuary.

As soon as all the gifts were sorted, work began on the building. Some men cut the shittim wood into boards of the right size for the sides and ends of the sanctuary. Others melted down the various metals, made molds for the castings, and began to beat the gold into thin sheets.

Some of the women spun thread for the fine linen, others spun goats' hair for one of the curtains, and still others

prepared the dyes being careful to get exactly the right colors.

Bezaleel himself made the ark, which was to contain the Ten Commandments and be the center of all the services. Because the glory of God would appear above it, he made it as perfect as he could. Of all the work he had ever done in his life, this was his finest. Never had he joined pieces of wood so exactly. Never had he beaten out gold so smoothly. There was not a crack, or a dent, or a rough place anywhere.

What a thrill he must have felt as he worked over the mercy seat! Fancy a mere man making a mercy seat for the great God of heaven! I am sure that Bezaleel polished and polished and polished that slab of solid gold until it shone like a mirror, without a mark or a scratch on it anywhere.

Above the mercy seat he put two golden angels, or "cherubim," which, with great skill and many hours of work, he beat out of solid gold.

When all was finished I imagine he stood back and looked at the beautiful, shining cabinet with honest pride, but still wishing that his poor hands might have made it better.

Then he worked on the golden altar of incense, the golden table for the shewbread, and the golden seven-branched candlestick. All were made with the same loving care and a keen desire that they might be pleasing to God.

Day by day the work went on. Those who were not able to help crowded around to watch as each piece of the tabernacle gradually took shape. Back in their tents at night—with no radios, no television sets, and no newspapers to amuse them—they must have talked about what they had seen, as people nowadays talk about a baseball game and the like. For the building of the tabernacle was the only thing of interest going on for hundreds of miles around. No doubt too, many went to Moses to ask him about the meaning of everything, and this gave him a chance to tell the story of God's plan of salvation over and over again.

At last, just six months from the day the work was begun, Bezaleel reported to his chief that all was finished. The tabernacle, the lovely golden furniture, the altar of brass for the burnt offerings that was to stand in front of the taber-

186

nacle, the long curtain that was to act as a sort of fence around everything, even the rich robes that Aaron and his sons were to wear—all were made just as Moses had asked.

"Well done, Bezaleel!" I am sure he said, for it was a wonderful thing the young man had accomplished out there in the desert, with not a single power tool to help him.

Then, just one year after Israel left Egypt, on the very morning of the first anniversary of their deliverance, "the tabernacle was reared up."

What excitement! Everybody was there to see it happen —men, women, and children, the whole million of them. There never had been such an audience to see a building go up before.

Then the furniture was moved in, Moses himself making sure that everything was put in its right place. He it was who put the two tables of the law in the ark and covered them with the mercy seat.

At last all was in order. So far as Moses could see, everything had been done exactly according to the pattern God had showed him in the mount. But would it please Him? Was He satisfied?

Suddenly, as everyone stood watching and wondering, "a cloud covered the tent of the congregation, and the glory of the Lord filled the tabernacle."

It must have been a tremendous sight. Everybody was thrilled, and so happy! But the happiest man of all was Bezaleel. He had tried so hard, he had done the best he knew how, and now God had been pleased to accept the work of his hands.

STORY 8

Blood on Their Toes

As NIGHT came on, the whole tabernacle seemed to be aglow, as if it were on fire. In the morning it was covered with a cloud. And "so it was alway: the cloud covered it by day, and the appearance of fire by night."

So Israel knew that God was with them. And it must have been very comforting when anybody in the camp felt sad or lonely, maybe in the middle of the night, to look toward the tabernacle and see that warm and friendly light. On the blackest night the desert was never quite dark.

During the next few weeks some exciting things happened. First came the big ceremony when Aaron and his sons were made priests of the sanctuary. Everybody was told to come and see this take place, for it was to be something very, very important.

It must have been a mighty crowd that gathered round the tabernacle that day. I can't imagine how all the thousands of people could possibly have had a good view. Maybe some

188

stood on the surrounding hillsides. But you may be sure the boys and girls got as close to the front line as they could.

And what did they see?

First of all, they saw six people come to the door of the tabernacle. In the center was Moses. In front of him stood Aaron and his four sons, Nadab, Abihu, Eleazar, and Ithamar. What interested everybody most, of course, was the fact that Aaron and his sons didn't have any clothes on—that is, nothing but their "linen breeches," or shorts.

"Whatever's going to happen?" they all wondered.

Then they saw Moses take water from a basin and begin to wash them. First Aaron, then Nadab, then Abihu, then Eleazar, and finally Ithamar.

"Why's he doing that?" the children asked their parents, who replied, "Because they are going to minister before God in the sanctuary, so they must be clean and pure all over—outside and inside."

Then Moses dressed Aaron in the robes that had been made for him. From a distance they looked very beautiful indeed, for they were of blue, purple, scarlet, and gold, just like the curtains of the sanctuary. Blue was to remind him—and the people—of God's perfection, revealed in His law. Scarlet was the color of sin, and purple the blending of the two in God's loving mercy.

On Aaron's chest Moses placed a handsome breastplate, each of its twelve jewels engraved with the name of one of the tribes of Israel, glittering in the bright morning sunshine.

On Aaron's shoulders Moses placed two large onyx stones, set in gold, each engraved with six names of the children of Israel. In this way Aaron was reminded that, as high priest, he must carry the burdens of the people both on his shoulders and on his heart—always.

When all these garments were in place Moses put a miter on Aaron's head, which had a solid gold band in front of it bearing the words, "HOLINESS TO THE LORD."

The shimmering gold seemed to make the words flash out across the camp, and no one, from the youngest to the oldest, could have had any doubt about what they meant. Aaron was to be a holy man, an example of holiness before all the people.

BLOOD ON THEIR TOES

While all this was going on, Nadab, Abihu, Eleazar, and Ithamar had been standing around watching what was happening to their father. At last, however, their turn came to be dressed. Going from one to the other of the boys, Moses put on each of them a coat, a girdle, and a bonnet. These were nothing like Aaron's, of course, but even so the Bible says they were "for glory and for beauty."

After this a bullock was brought to where the group was standing, and Aaron and his sons all laid their hands on the head of the struggling animal as a mark of their confession of sin. Then Moses slew the animal and sprinkled its blood around the altar.

Then a ram was brought. Again Aaron and his sons laid their hands on the animal's head, after which the ram was killed and its blood sprinkled on the altar.

Next another ram was brought, called the "ram of con-

secration." Once more—for the third time—the five placed their hands in the same position, as though laying all their sins on the animal. But this time something different happened. Instead of sprinkling the blood of the ram on the altar, Moses put some of it "upon the tip of Aaron's right ear, and upon the thumb of his right hand, and upon the great toe of his right foot."

After that he came to the four boys and put some of the blood "upon the tip of their right ear, and upon the thumbs of their right hands, and upon the great toes of their right feet."

The children looking on must have thought, "What a strange thing for Moses to do!"

But it was not so strange, after all.

Blood on the ear meant that they were not to listen to evil. They were to keep their thoughts pure, clean, and holy.

Blood on the thumb of the right hand meant that they were to use their hands for noble purposes. They were to be consecrated to doing good, helping the poor and needy, and building the kingdom of God.

Blood on their toes meant that they were to walk in the ways of righteousness. They were to follow the path of God's commandments, never wandering into places where God would not want them to go.

In short, it all meant a complete consecration to God and to the holy work He wanted them to do. We should be consecrated like this too—with the blood of Jesus on our ears, our thumbs, and our toes.